My 50-Day Pentecost in the Holy Land

First printing April 2024

Library of Congress Cataloging-in-Publication Data

Ceremuga, George
my 50-day pentecost in the holy land / by dr. george ceremuga

Paperback ISBN: 9798323089215
Hardcover ISBN: 9798323089307

Published by AR PRESS, an American Real Publishing Company
Roger L. Brooks, Publisher
roger@incubatemedia.us
americanrealpublishing.com

Interior design by Eva Myrick, MSCP

Printed in the U.S.A.

MY 50-DAY PENTECOST IN THE HOLY LAND

DR. GEORGE J. CEREMUGA

My 50-Day Pentecost in the Holy Land is dedicated to all people who have lived or visited this "Terra Sancta" past, present and future. The Holy Land is remarkably beautiful—including its people, history, and diverse landscapes. Thank you to my new Jewish, Muslim, Druze, and Christian brothers and sisters that I proudly call friends. We have the power to unite all in love, for God is love.

TABLE OF CONTENTS

FOREWORD

God told Moses on Mount Sinai that every seven years the land of Israel must lay fallow, and Jews are forbidden to work it. "For six years you may sow your land and gather in its produce. But the seventh year you shall let the land lie untilled and unharvested, that the poor among you may eat of it and beasts of the field may eat what the poor leave" (Exodus 23:10-11). This is called the Shmita, a year to give the land time to reconnect with God, so that it can reach its full potential in the next year and for years to come.

God's timing is perfect. We, at Dr. George J, have toiled in the fields of Holistic Health and Healing and are blessed to complete our seventh year together in 2023. During our "Shmita" or a year to give (July 2022 - June 2023) we were honored to share the gospel message of salvation through healthcare all for the glory of God, internationally through our book, *God Loves the Children*. I had the privilege to spend six weeks in the Holy Land and travel solo prior to the culmination of our Shmita with a group pilgrimage. Altogether, I was blessed with a fifty-three day stay in the land of milk and honey filled with the power of the Holy Spirit.

INTRODUCTION

I was cautioned by many prior to my trip to the Holy Land in the spring of 2023. “It is too dangerous. Be careful. Are you sure you should go?” I like to make informed decisions. I have no trust in the “fake news” or the political systems. Sadly, with the violence in our own country, I felt quite safe embarking on this trip of a lifetime. As a person that enjoys traveling and experiencing diverse culture, history, landscapes and most importantly the people, I hit a home run!

I enjoyed my daily walks and public transportation filled with conversations with people from all over the world. The Mediterranean food was equally nutritious and delicious. A few highlights included: Dance night at the St. Louis French Hospital, Pentecost in the “West Bank,” bike riding around the Sea of Galilee, renewing my baptismal promise in the Jordan River, traveling throughout the Golan Heights, and giving honor in Jesus’s hometown of Nazareth at the Sisters of St Joseph Catholic School teaching the Creator model of healthcare to the seventh and eighth grade students.

My experience in the Holy Land amongst us

common people: Jews, Muslims, Christians, and Druze is that we all love the same God and desire peace within the "Holy Land." We all are descendants of Abraham and share a common lineage and glorify the same God. While floating on my back in the Dead Sea on June 21, 2023, the Holy Spirit whispered to me the solution for peace in the Holy Land. The solution to a complex problem was quite enlightening.

CHAPTER 1

MY 50 DAY PENTECOST BEGINS

As I made last-minute preparations for my seven-week sojourn to the Holy Land, I felt both excitement and peace for this adventure. I purposely left weeks unplanned to allow room for the Holy Spirit to work. Patience is the companion to wisdom (St. Augustine). The Holy Spirit filled in all the "gaps," and I would not have changed a thing looking back. As I have been journaling daily for ten years, it has helped me in so many ways to connect with God and keep grounded in my thoughts. I will rely on my journal, plethora of pictures, and most importantly the Holy Spirit to share this experience.

I woke up on Tuesday, May second, went for a

run, attended mass and caught a ride to the airport from a friend. I would be in the air for a total of sixteen hours on three different flights. The Rapid City, South Dakota to Dallas, Texas flight was two hours, Dallas to New York City (NYC) was three hours and NYC to Tel Aviv eleven hours. It is all a mindset. I was excited and grateful for this opportunity. Gratitude is the antidote to negative thinking. Who was God going to introduce to me on my travels? As your thoughts go, so shall you be (Proverbs 23:7). Choose wisely!

My flight to JFK airport in NYC went very smoothly. At gate three in the JFK terminal, I looked up at the monitor and noticed that my flight was boarding in eight minutes. Yes, American Airlines flight 146 to Tel Aviv-Yafo (Jaffa) was about to board. I was amongst many Orthodox Jews and their young families. I shared in the excitement for this was my first trip to the "Holy Land." I was blessed to meet many wonderful people enroute and many fellow passengers earnestly said with big smiles "You are going to have a wonderful time in the Holy Land." They confirmed what I already felt inside.

I sat next to Ghabit, a young Jewish woman living in New York City in transition from a non-profit job in Israel. Her parents lived in Jerusalem, and she was going to visit them for a few weeks. She was exactly who God wanted me to witness to. She was struggling with a few issues in her life, and I offered a non-judgmental ear and the love of Jesus Christ. I gifted her a copy of *God Loves the Children* and personalized it with, “May the blessings of the Lord be upon you. Lead with Love, George.” She was the first recipient of our book on the Holy Land tour, and she was incredibly grateful for the gift. Between visiting with Ghabit, eating, and sleeping, the time “flew” by.

I arrived in the Holy Land at 4:00 p.m. Israel time. It was a breeze going through customs at the Ben Gurion airport, and I was soon negotiating the price with Sean for a taxi to my Airbnb stay for the first two nights outside of Tel Aviv. It seemed like the going rate for my destination was 150 Shekels or (NIS= New Israeli Shekel). Four shekels was equivalent to one US dollar. My hosts, Itsik and Reli, were waiting for me with refreshments and the warmth of their lovely home. We visited for hours and then enjoyed a Mediterranean meal before I went to bed at 11:00 p.m. With a full belly and the blessings of the Lord, I slept well.

The next day, my adoptive hosts invited me to attend a museum tour in Tel Aviv. Tel Aviv means “The Hill of Spring.” We drove to a “park and ride” lot and then rode a bus into the city. I enjoyed the talented and creative artistic pieces, especially the outdoor cocoon that we could play in. We had supper at a local Jewish restaurant with a fabulous array of fermented vegetables, hummus, whole grains, chicken, and seafood. After supper, I walked to the mall in the Yehud district and bought some dates for my travels to Jerusalem tomorrow by train. We had more delightful conversations and I shared with them a copy of *God Loves the Children*. We respected each other's faith boundaries, and my first impression of the Holy Land was blessed! I highly recommend staying at Reli and Itsik's Airbnb in Yehud outside of Tel Aviv.

CHAPTER 2

THE HOLY LAND RICH AND VARIABLE

"Geographically, the Holy Land is rich in complexity, featuring a coastal plain, a semi-mountainous hill country in Judah and Galilee, the wide valley of Jezreel, and a fertile region in Galilee that sloped down to the Sea of Galilee. A tremendous rift in the earth makes up the southern part of the Jordan River near Jericho and the Dead Sea. There is the deep desert of Judah, which swings around south and west to the Negev. West of the Jordan is the steppe and the dry, barren Golan Heights. There is the snow-covered Mount Herman to the northwest and the rich groves of cypress trees in Lebanon to the northeast. Israel is similar in size to New Jersey with a population approaching ten million people.

It is a land of great variety, and the terrain is incredibly complex. This brings about dramatic, localized effects on the weather and vegetation. Fertile valleys can give way to deep desert within miles. Just to the west of Jerusalem are the green hills of the Judean Hill country that resemble the Appalachians. Yet just to the east of Jerusalem, over the Mount of Olives, begins a 3,500-foot descent into the deep and extremely dry desert of the Dead Sea and Jericho. At 1,400 feet below sea level, the Dead Sea is the lowest place on earth" **(1)**.

The weather during my fifty-day Pentecost in the Holy Land was hot and dry. I witnessed rain only on a few occasions, and it was short-lived. Jerusalem was more temperate because of its elevation and highs ranged from twenty-four to thirty-two degrees Celsius (seventy-five to ninety degrees Fahrenheit). At the higher elevations the nights cooled off nicely. The Judean desert, Dead Sea, and Sea of Galilee would routinely reach one hundred degrees or more. This Mediterranean climate does see snow in the winter months at higher elevations.

CHAPTER 3

JERUSALEM—THE OLD CITY

There are no coincidences in life, only *Godcidents*! The name of my taxi driver from my homestay to the train station was Shalom Shalom (Peace Peace). Reli negotiated a price of 120 shekels and after we exchanged hugs and goodbyes, I was off to the train station at the Ben Gurion airport. The high-speed train ride was twenty-five minutes and cost twenty NIS or five dollars. While waiting for the train, I visited with Pastor Steve and his wife Joy from Dayton, Ohio. They received the third copy of *God Loves the Children.* I met them again at the end of the day as I visited the Notre Dame Center Hotel in Jerusalem after mass.

The train drops you off at the Yitzhak Navon

Station in the middle of Jerusalem. From there, I caught the light rail which runs with many convenient stops throughout Jerusalem. At the light rail station, with the assistance of a young Jewish woman, I first bought a Rav-Kav, a public transit smartcard that would be my primary means of transportation during my fifty-day Pentecost in the Holy Land. My stop was at the City Center, a mere ten-minute ride. With a backpack, duffle bag, and roller bag, I made the short walk from the City Center to the Dar Mamilla guest house on the premises of the St. Vincent DePaul convent.

I arrived at noon on May fifth and was greeted warmly and oriented by Beatrice from the staff of Pro Terra Sancta. Room number sixteen would be my home for the next twenty-one days. Outside my room was a courtyard where the St. Vincent DePaul sisters ran a kindergarten and a home for mentally and physically challenged adults. Most afternoons, music and dancing were offered to the residents. There was a large, shared kitchen and living room area for common use. The refrigerator and pantry were well stocked with breakfast items such as eggs, cheese, yogurt, fresh bread, and fruit. The location Koresh St 16, Jerusalem, 9414403, Israel was close and convenient to the New and Jaffa Gates of the Old City. It also was a five-minute walk to the Notre Dame Center where I would attend daily mass singing in the choir and serving as a lector.

Prior to my arrival in the Holy Land, I was looking for opportunities to volunteer as a physician. I spoke to Alex, the CEO of the St. Louis French Hospital to coordinate a visit. The hospital was a short distance from the Dar Mamilla. On my first day in Jerusalem, I stopped unannounced and was greeted by Lamesha, a kind receptionist. She took me to the chapel and parlor room as I waited for Alex. He was very sincere and open to the Creator model of healthcare message within *God Loves the Children.* We enjoyed a delightful conversation about spiritual health especially in end-of-life care. Is there a better gift than to share the path to salvation?

This hospital now serves as a palliative care and extended care facility, an ideal setting to spread the gospel message of salvation. It is my belief that all people, whether they have called upon the name of Jesus Christ or not will see His face upon death. "For anyone that calls upon the name of the Lord will be saved" (Romans 10:13). Alex, an Arab Christian appreciated our discussion and the seed planted. His challenge was that the hospital served Jews, Muslims, and Christians and the Israeli government controlled the narrative on religion.

I was in my glory as everywhere I walked there

were freshly squeezed juice stands. My first "juice" was pomegranate, grapefruit, and orange juice. It was delicious. You feel healthy when you eat and drink healthily. During my stay in the Holy Land the beet, carrot, apple and ginger juice would become my favorite. I drank one to two of these refreshing juices daily. I became a preferred customer of many of the vendors.

I visited the Notre Dame Center where we would be staying during our pilgrimage June sixteenth through the twenty-fourth. This beautiful hotel with a rooftop restaurant and ground floor Café Bistro would be my second home while in Jerusalem. They offered daily mass at 6:30 p.m. and mass on Sunday. I enjoyed singing with the choir and filling in as a lector when needed.

I wasted no time in arranging a meeting with Sister Simone at the St. Vincent de Paul preschool and kindergarten. The school opened its doors to many refugees and there were eight different nationalities amongst the 230 children. I was able to gather some of the children and sing to them, "May the blessings of the Lord be upon you." The children were happy and well cared for. I almost jumped into the playground of balls with the children. They were having too much fun. "Return to that of a child to enter the kingdom of God" (Matthew 18:3). Sister Simone who is from Lebanon graciously accepted a copy of *God Loves the Children*. I ended my tour of the school by singing to her as well. She smiled, chuckled, and blushed, all predictable responses.

Now it was time to start exploring the Old City. Today, the Old City is divided into four uneven quarters, the Muslim Quarter, the Christian Quarter, the Armenian Quarter, and the Jewish Quarter. A fifth area, the Temple Mount is sacred to both Muslims and Jews. Known to Muslims as Al-Aqsa, the Temple Mount is home to the Dome of the Rock, the Al-Aqsa Mosque and once was the site of two Jewish Temples. The Old City is a 0.35 square mile walled area that has an estimated population of 38,000 people with Muslims being the majority, followed by Jews, Christians and Armenians. For a geographically small area, it is packed with shops, restaurants, schools, churches, mosques, and synagogues. Highlights for me were the old Arab market with a plethora of produce and souvenir items, the Dome of the Rock on the Temple Mount, the Tower of David Museum, the Western Wall, and the Holy Sepulcher.

"The Dome of the Rock is a Islamic shrine at the center of the Al-Aqsa Mosque compound on the Temple Mount in the Old City of Jerusalem. Its initial construction was undertaken in 691–692 AD, and it has since been situated on top of the site of the Second Jewish Temple, which was built in 516 BC to replace the destroyed Solomon's Temple and rebuilt by Herod the Great. This temple was destroyed by the Romans in 70 AD. The original dome collapsed in 1015 and was rebuilt in 1022–23. The Dome of the Rock is the world's oldest surviving work of Islamic architecture." Bahgat, an elderly Muslim man approached me and offered to take me on a tour. His knowledge of this holy site and of Jerusalem was most welcomed and a blessing. I was most impressed with the size of the Temple Mount as it is thirty-six acres and contains a beautiful park with many access points to the Old City **(2)**.

The Tower of David Museum is in the restored ancient Citadel of Jerusalem at the entrance to the Old City. The museum tells the story of the city through history using models, displays and multimedia so that the timeline of the city comes to life. The exhibition takes the visitor on a journey through 3,000 years of history **(3)**. We spent an entire afternoon mesmerized by all the interactive models and multi-media as well as walking the grounds of this great citadel. The name "Tower of David" was first used for the Herodian tower in the fifth century AD by the Byzantine Christians, who believed the site to be the palace of King David. They borrowed the name "Tower of David" from the Song of Songs, attributed to Solomon, King David's son, who wrote:

"Thy neck is like the Tower of David built with turrets, whereon there hang a thousand shields, all the armor of the mighty men" **(4)**.

The Western Wall is a place of prayer and pilgrimage sacred to the Jewish people. It is the only remains of the retaining wall surrounding the Temple Mount, the site of the First and Second Temples of Jerusalem, held to be uniquely holy by the ancient Jews. The First Temple was destroyed by the Babylonians in 587–586 BC, and the Second Temple was destroyed by the Romans in 70 AD. Jews lament the destruction of the Temple and pray for its restoration at the Western Wall. It has long been a custom to insert slips of paper with wishes or prayers on them into the wall's cracks **(5)**. I visited this sacred site four times during my Holy Land Pentecost. There is a partition wall dividing access to the Western Wall, one side for men and the other for women. I was called by the Lord to go to the Western Wall on the eve of my departure and pray. The events that unfolded at the Western Wall that evening were miraculous and to keep you in suspense will be shared chronologically in Chapter twenty-seven. As you will soon read, there is power in the name of Jesus!

The Church of the Holy Sepulcher, or Church of the Resurrection, is a church in the Christian Quarter of the Old City of Jerusalem. It is the holiest site for Christians in the world, as it has been the most important pilgrimage site for Christianity since the fourth century. According to traditions dating back to the fourth century, it contains two sites considered holy in Christianity: the site where Jesus was crucified, at a place known as Calvary or Golgotha, and Jesus's empty tomb, which is where he was buried and resurrected. I attended mass in both Latin and Eastern Rite as well as Greek Orthodox within the Church of the Holy Sepulcher.

One early morning a few of us pilgrims walked to the Holy Sepulcher for mass and to honor this holy site. Enroute, we met a priest named Father Anastasis from the United States. He greeted us warmly and confirmed we were heading in the right direction. As we entered the Holy Sepulcher, we visited and paid homage to the Golgotha (site of Christ's crucifixion). We then visited the stone of the anointing where Jesus's body was anointed with oil and perfumes prior to being placed in the tomb. As we entered the tomb of Jesus, you first enter the anteroom called the Chapel of the Angel. Then, you enter through a small opening to His tomb into a small room that can accommodate four people at a time. Indeed, a powerful and prayerful moment!

Then, our colleague, Ayn, asked, "Where is Christ's resurrection represented?" Google confirmed the answer given to us earlier by the Holy

Spirit inspired meeting with Father Anastasis. The rotunda in the Church of the Holy Sepulcher is called the Anastasis or Resurrection. With great delight, we smiled and said, “That was you God!” Thank you, Father Anastasis, for our *Godcident* moment!

Next, I visited The Church of All Nations, also known as the Church or Basilica of the Agony. It is a Roman Catholic church located on the Mount of Olives in East Jerusalem, next to the Garden of Gethsemane. The garden was full of beautiful flowers and olive trees that were recently carbon dated at 900 years old **(6)**. We were blessed on our pilgrimage to attend mass inside the Basilica of the Agony at a section of bedrock where Jesus is said to have prayed before his arrest.

CHAPTER 4

ABU GHOSH: "VILLAGE OF WOODS"

Abu Ghosh is an Arab-Israeli community in Israel, located ten kilometers (6.2 mi) west of Jerusalem on the Tel Aviv–Jerusalem highway and is situated 610–720 meters above sea level. Abu Ghosh is identified with the biblical site of Kiryat Ye'arim (Hebrew meaning: "Village of Woods"), the town to which the Ark of the Covenant was taken after it had left Beth-shemesh **(7)** (1 Samuel 6:1-7:2).

According to Christian tradition, Jesus and his disciples did a lot of walking. Now pilgrims who want to walk in Jesus's footsteps can do so on a new trail called the Emmaus Trail, which could be the road that Cleopas and the unknown disciple walked from Jerusalem to Emmaus after the death of Jesus.

According to the Gospel of Luke, as they walked, they discussed the events that led to the crucifixion. At some point Jesus, who had been resurrected, appeared to them but they didn't recognize Him. When they arrived at Emmaus, which today is part of Ayalon Park near Latrun, they invited Jesus to stay the night with them. It was only then, when they sat and ate together, that they recognized Him. Our last morning of the Pilgrimage was spent in Emmaus, and I will share more in Chapter twenty-eight.

Pilgrims can walk the new 18-km (11-mile) Emmaus Trail that now goes from the Saxum Visitor Center in Abu Ghosh, which has exhibits on Christianity, and ends at the monastery of Emmaus Nicopolis. The whole walk takes five to six hours at a modest pace **(8).**

I toured the Saxon Visitor Center as the guest of Father Fernando Monge. I was most impressed with its outdoor chronology of the Old Testament. Father Monge and I both met looking for the start of the Emmaus trail. As we introduced ourselves to one another, we noticed the start of the trail was directly below us. Father Monge is from Spain and serving in Austria. He also has two brothers that are priests. We walked three hours together on the Emmaus trail with Jesus and stopped and shared our lunches as we sat on an old couch along the trail. It was along the trail that Father Monge pointed out in the distance where the Ark of the Covenant was taken per 1 Samuel 6:1-7:2. We enjoyed our conversation in English and in Spanish. We had Jesus to ourselves the entire time. We joyfully recited a bilingual rosary, my part in English and his in Spanish as we were blessed to spend time together as brothers in Christ. Father Monge appreciated a signed copy of *God Loves the Children*. I have gained another brother in Christ along my path to salvation!

I then proceeded walking back towards the town center. I noticed an elderly Muslim woman getting off a bus with more bags of groceries than hands to carry. I instinctively picked up two bags of groceries not knowing what I was going to do with them. She smiled and said, “follow me.” We walked a short distance down the hill and entered her courtyard and home. Her name was Gharmet, and her sister was Siom. They offered me Arabic coffee with crackers, then they put me to work. We shucked artichokes for an hour. They kept repeating, “thank you very much” and my reply with a smile in Arabic was, “Afwan” (welcome).

After making myself useful, I politely excused myself and caught bus #185 back to the central bus station in Jerusalem. The bus ride was approximately twenty-five minutes. I then hopped on the light rail and was back to my room in short order. I had time to shower, rest, and then attend the 6:30 p.m. daily mass. Indeed, I experienced a full and abundant day in the kingdom of God. The next day, I was invited to St. Joseph's Catholic School to talk about "God Loves the Children" and the Creator model of healthcare. Thank you, Jesus!

CHAPTER 5

ST JOSEPH'S SCHOOL

I was invited a week prior by Sister Frida, an administrator at the St. Joseph's school located on St. George Street in the Old City, to present to her 256 children at recess on Monday, May 15, 2023. I awoke early that morning and made the fifteen-minute walk to the Holy Sepulcher. I attended mass with a group from Guatemala in the Golgotha Chapel. I attempted to gain entrance into the tomb where Jesus was buried but was unable to enter because of another mass in progress.

As I entered the school's courtyard, I was met with the energy of 256 middle school students. These children were on fire for the Holy Spirit and well-behaved. I gave them an overview of the Creator model of healthcare five pillars of wellness and then I taught them a dance hopping from foot-to-foot singing, "Salaam, Shalom, Peace." I know this "big child" enjoyed his time with the children, and by their dancing, laughter, and chatter, I surmised they did as well.

A few days later, I again went to mass at the Holy Sepulcher. On my way back through the Old City, I was addressed by three separate students walking to school that recognized me from my presentation a few days earlier at the St. Joseph's school. They smiled when they saw me and joyfully proclaimed, "Salaam, Shalom, Peace." These three encounters were signals of grace given to me by God. Put God first, Jesus did, and he will continue to bless you abundantly. These are Holy Moments made possible by the Holy Spirit. The spirit of truth is the Holy Spirit. The Holy Spirit reveals God's personal love, opens our heart to scripture, opens our eyes to see each other as "Jesus in disguise," and reveals our destiny. Thanks be to God!

CHAPTER 6

BETHLEHEM: HOUSE OF BREAD

In Hebrew, the city's name is pronounced "Beit-lehem. "Beit" means house and "Lechem" means bread. Thus, Bethlehem means "House of Bread" **(9)**. On Thursday, May eighteenth, I awoke eager to start my day. Over my toast, yogurt, and fruit breakfast, I visited with Pete and Joy from Chicago, and Laura and Elena from Italy. My destination for the day was Bethlehem via bus #234 from the bus station below the New Gate. The bus ride was fifteen minutes with an Israeli Defense Force (IDF) security check along the way. Bethlehem is in the occupied West Bank.

Mandatory security checks occur returning from the West Bank, although random checks occur entering as well. I took a taxi from checkpoint 300 to meet Anita at the Pro Terra Sancta (Holy Land). This is where I met Iyad, a most pleasant tour guide. I had the pleasure of meeting Iyad a week prior on a separate visit to Bethlehem. He has an award-winning smile and a wonderful business model. "After I take you to the places that you would like to see, if you enjoyed your experience, you decide how much to pay me." With his personality and charm, he is quite successful. I would use his expert guide service on a "road trip" throughout Samaria culminating with supper on May 28th, the Feast of Pentecost with his family. I will cover this experience with delight in an upcoming chapter.

Pro Terra Sancta is an organization that promotes and implements projects for the conservation and enhancement of local communities and assists in humanitarian emergencies. It is an Italian based non-profit organization with an international mission to foster bonds between the Holy Land and the world **(10)**. At Pro Terra Sancta, I was very impressed with their outreach to the vulnerable populations in providing water and electricity. I was glad to witness their robust support system in place to create jobs and promote a vast array of handmade crafts.

Anita then took me to the Elderly Women's Home that served as a residential facility much like our nursing homes. The director, Suzy, was a phenomenal woman with a huge warm smile. I met all the residents and was invited to lunch and a seventy-seventh birthday celebration for Souad. We all joined in a chorus of happy birthday and offered Souad a blessing on her special day. I then visited a daycare adjacent to the women's home and offered a prayer and blessing for the children and staff.

My final visit was to the Hogar Niño Dios (Home of God's Children). The Hogar Niño Dios is a welcome house near the Basilica of the Nativity that hosts children and young people with physical and mental disabilities, orphans, or those from poor families. This home is run by a small group of nuns with an amazing group of volunteers from all over the world. I was able to meet and play with all the children and offer prayers of healing and blessings for each. They enjoyed me singing, "May the blessing of the Lord be upon you. We bless you in the name of the Lord. May the blessings of the Lord be upon you, we bless you in the name of the Lord!" I thanked Anita for her kindness and the opportunity to witness many servants of the Lord in action.

At the bus stop, we were informed that the buses were not operational due to Israel Peace Day. I took a taxi back to Jerusalem with Juliet, a volunteer from France and her mother Andronese who was visiting the Holy Land and a psychologist at a Paris Addiction Hospital. We exchanged contact information and offered each other blessings for safe travels.

CHAPTER 7

EIN KAREM AND HADASSAH-EIN KAREM MEDICAL CENTER

On Sunday, May twenty first, I rode the light rail to the last stop westward to catch bus number twenty-seven to Ein Karem. It was a short bus ride as Ein Karem is a suburb of Jerusalem. The bus stop for Ein Karem was at the hospital. I stopped at the hospital and arranged a tour for the next day. I then proceeded to the Russian Orthodox Gorensky Convent nestled within a beautiful campus of trees, shrubs, and flowers. I timed it perfectly for the outdoor mass at the Cathedral of All Russian Saints, as the priest and congregation prayed at each corner of the church. The priest sprinkled Holy Water with a whisk onto the faithful at each corner as well. The songs and prayers were beautiful and uplifting. Father was quite generous with the “living water” reminding us that the Spirit is the living water welling up in us to eternal life.

After mass I was invited by Kate to attend a celebration serving a delicious plant-based meal. At the celebration, I met Roman who was originally from St. Petersburg, Russia and now in preparation for becoming a monk. We visited the John the Baptist Russian Orthodox Church, Church of the Visitation (Mary’s visit to her cousin Elizabeth), and Mary’s Spring. It was on my walk to Mary’s Spring that I met Hasti, a pleasant woman who appeared to be in her sixties. I introduced myself after greeting her with, “This is the day that the Lord has made.” She smiled and then replied, “I do not believe in God.” We exchanged pleasantries and marveled about the beautiful flowers and scenery in Ein Karem. I mentioned that it was a *Godcident* that we met. God always brings his people together for His glory. She was not convinced. Hasti lives with her spouse in Caesarea Maritime on the Mediterranean Sea. I said goodbye with, “May the blessings of the Lord be upon you.” She smiled and we went our separate ways.

Now let's fast forward two weeks ahead as I am walking through the Old City of Nazareth, two hours from Ein Karem. I hear a voice, “Hi, how are you?” I turn and Hasti is standing with her husband with a big smile on her face. "I bet you are going to call this a *Godcident*, too?" I replied, "Hasti, you bet I am!" They had made the drive from their home in Caesarea Maritime to spend the day in Nazareth. With much delight we visited in the market, and I felt humbled and blessed that God used me to plant a seed in their hearts.

I walked back to the Hadassah-Ein Karem Medical Center and saw a sign for the International Medicine Department. As I entered the department, I met a pleasant woman named Drora. I introduced myself to her and told her I was interested in a sabbatical to practice medicine in the Holy Land. I met the right person. Drora was the head of the Human Resource Department for the hiring of physicians. She took the time to call a physician friend, Dr Sara, and we met in the hospital food court. I explained that I was a missionary disciple spreading the gospel message of salvation through healthcare. Both women were Jewish and when asked my religion, I responded with, "I follow the religion of the Perfect Jew." Our short time together was cordial as they both showed interest in my Holistic Health and Healing workshops for the hospital staff. I made it back to Jerusalem in time to attend mass. Thank you, God, for a wonderful day and for the people that you brought into my life.

The next morning, I followed the same routine

traveling to the Hadassah-Ein Karem Medical Center for my tour. I was met by Marjion at the visitor's center inside the medical center. She introduced me to Shira (Hebrew for "my song") who gave me a tour of the twelve Chagall stain-glassed windows in the Abbell Synagogue. These beautiful windows represent the twelve tribes of Israel. Marc Chagall, a Russian Jew, wrote on February 6, 1962: "This is my modest gift to the Jewish people who have dreamt of biblical love, friendship and of peace among all people. This is my gift to that people, who lived here thousands of years among other Semitic people."

I then was fortunate to have Nicole guide me on a tour of the rest of the hospital. She explained that Hadassah means "myrtle tree" and is associated with peace, love, and prosperity. Hadassah is also Hebrew for Esther. Queen Esther saved her people from death while exiled in Persia (KJV: Esther Chapters 5&6). In the Pediatric wing, Nicole mentioned that Hadassah is also known as Esther of Persia with a faithful devotion to God with her sweet and docile nature. Hadassah was a Jewish woman who became the queen of Persia and used her influence to save her people from destruction. The story of Hadassah is told in the Book of Esther, which is read during the Purim Jewish joyous festival. Hadassah/Esther is viewed as a heroine in

Jewish tradition and is celebrated for her courage and resilience. She pointed out that hanging high in the main entrance of the medical center in Hebrew, Arabic, and English is “Healing Our World Together Since 1912.” Nicole was an encyclopedia of information as she had worked at the medical center for almost four decades. I was able to visit the healing gardens and the inpatient urology and orthopedic floor. The medical center employs 7,000 people: 2,100 nurses and 1,300 physicians, with 14,000 babies delivered annually and one million patients served. Many languages are spoken amongst the diverse staff that is two-thirds Jewish and one-third Muslim and Christian in a medical center that prides itself as a place for healing for all God’s people.

CHAPTER 8

THE OLD CITY WITH DR JOHN AND GLORIA

Tuesday, May twenty-third, I was inspired by the Holy Spirit to attend mass at thc Holy Sepulcher. I was blessed to enter the tomb of Jesus and offer my honor and praise giving thanks to our resurrected Savior! I then proceeded to the Church of St. Anne, Mary's mother. On my way there, a dove flew right in front of me and landed on a ledge to nest with his mate. Thank you, Holy Spirit, for this signal of grace. Beautiful praise and worship songs were being sung by various pilgrim groups inside the church of St. Anne.

The Bethesda pool is located outside the church where Jesus healed the paralytic of thirty-eight years: "Rise, pick up your mat and walk" (NIV, John 5:8). Then I made my way through the Jewish

Quarter viewing ancient Roman columns built before the birth of Jesus. A Jewish Synagogue was visible across the street with a purple Jacaranda tree offering a beautiful accent.

I was introduced to Dr John Ben-Daniel and his wife Gloria. I met them in his office at the St. Louis French Hospital. John is originally from England and Gloria from Mexico. They met in Israel where John is a family physician. John became aware of his Jewish roots later in life and he and Gloria have written a book about the Book of Revelation. This book is the culmination of thirty years dedicated to the study of Revelation and its setting in the New and Old Testaments. The book is titled, *Saint John and the Book of Revelation from Essenes to End-Times.* I found the final chapter to be the most clear and concise explanation of Revelation 12-22 and end time prophecy that I have read leading up to the second coming of Jesus Christ, final judgment and renewal of creation.

John and Gloria invited me to their home on St. Francis Street in the Christian Quarter of the Old City. We had a delightful visit culminating with a delicious plant-based meal of fruit and nuts. I found the papaya to be especially mouthwatering and delicious. We gifted each other books and John also recommended that I read *Turtles all the way down-Vaccine Science and Myth.* I am currently not a vaccine advocate, and it is my opinion that the Covid-19 vaccine is a biological weapon and is being used as a crime against humanity. Over my thirty-year medical career, I have witnessed many harmful vaccine side effects with some permanent and deadly. There is a better way through the Creator model of healthcare five pillars of wellness, which is lifestyle medicine.

After spending the afternoon with my new friends, I attended mass at the Notre Dame Center and then walked next door to the St. Louis French Hospital to join the weekly Arabic music to dance with patients and staff. It was a joy to see the smiles of patients and staff enjoying this outside venue in the fresh air.

CHAPTER 9

BACK TO BETHLEHEM FOR A RADIO INTERVIEW

On May twenty-fifth, I was invited by Paul Calvert with Radio Hayah (life) and Cross Rhythms International for an interview discussing the *God Loves the Children* book and the Creator model of healthcare spreading the gospel message of salvation. God never intended medicine or the path to salvation to be complicated or messy. The book simplifies both. We also talked about the social, economic, and religious challenges in the Holy Land and a proposal to bring the Jesus of Nazareth International College of Osteopathic Medicine to Nazareth. A few days later, I traveled to Nazareth and was able to share this vision with different groups of medical providers and community leaders. The full twelve-minute radio interview can be heard at https://youtu.be/XPRQLcm7YLA.

I then spent time in Bethlehem at the St. Mary's Syrian Catholic Church before visiting Sami the coffee and tea man with his award-winning smile and personality. Sami's magnetism and entrepreneurial business was featured in the *Christian Century* December 2022. I joined Haytham, a Palestinian film maker for some tea and conversation. Sami prepared me fresh mint, lemon, cinnamon, and parsley tea. The first was so tasty, he gladly gave me a refill. Haytham and I discussed collaborating on a documentary, "The healing power of God." As I gifted him a signed copy of our daily inspirations book, *All for the Glory of God*, Haytham mentioned he was an atheist. With much appreciation and gratitude, he accepted my gift. Thank you, Holy Spirit, for the prompt and the courage to do your will.

After tea and conversation, I asked Sami where I could get a haircut. Sami walked me across the street to meet Mohammed. I met Mohammed's two children, and he gave me one of the best haircuts that I have ever received. I told him it would become the costliest haircut if I had to return every six weeks. Without warning he even used a BIC lighter to singe the ear hairs. At times, I felt the heat but was never burned. That was quite an experience. This I shared at my barber shop upon my return to the United States and they were amazed. They all started to watch this on YouTube with curiosity.

I returned late in the afternoon to Jerusalem and decided to have an early supper at the Versavee (Savior's Way) restaurant. This was becoming my favorite restaurant just inside the Jaffa gate in the Old City. As I entered the courtyard, I stopped at the fresh juice stand and complimented the owner for his "fruit of the spirit" and "who am I in Christ" signs with scripture behind him. "Let all you do be done in love." (1 Corinthians 16:14). I enjoyed my cocktail of orange, ginger, and pomegranate juice. I ordered hummus and a Greek salad with fried cheese and a glass of red wine. The day was fabulous and blessed.

As I was about to leave, two young adults approached me and asked me where I was from. Delicia was from the United Kingdom and Jacob from the United States. They also were missionary disciples and prayed over me and my ministry. They prophesied that God would bless me with increased resources to teach young people who will be attracted to my message of love. "You will heal many people in the name of love." Wow, that was a Holy Moment! Thank you, Jesus!

CHAPTER 10

THE "OCCUPIED" WEST BANK

"The Occupied West Bank is a landlocked territory near the coast of the Mediterranean in the Holy Land that forms the main bulk of the Palestinian territories. It is bordered by Jordan and the Dead Sea to the east and by Israel to the south, west, and north. It has been under Israeli military and civil occupation since the 1967 Arab-Israeli War. Since the Oslo II Accord was signed in 1995, its area has been split into 165 Palestinian enclaves that are under total or partial civil administration by the Palestinian National Authority (PNA) and a contiguous area containing 230 Israeli settlements into which Israeli law is "pipelined."

The West Bank includes East Jerusalem. Israel

administers the West Bank excluding East Jerusalem as the Judea and Samaria Area district, through the Israeli Civil Administration. It has an estimated population of 2,747,943 Palestinians, and over 670,000 Israeli settlers live in the West Bank, of which approximately 220,000 live in East Jerusalem. The international community considers Israeli settlements in the West Bank and East Jerusalem to be illegal under international law, though Israel disputes this. Alongside the self-governing Gaza Strip, the Israeli-occupied West Bank and East Jerusalem are claimed by the State of Palestine as its sovereign territory, and thus remain a flashpoint in the Israeli–Palestinian conflict" **(11).**

On May twenty-sixth, I took my fourth trip to the West Bank and third trip to Bethlehem in my first three weeks in the Holy Land. I find the Muslim people to be very kind and hospitable. I have been invited into homes for coffee, biscuits, shucking artichokes and insightful conversation. It was in Bethlehem that I met my "favorite" tour guide Iyad, whose name means "reinforcement," who would take me two hours north into the heart of Samaria to meet Madji, who would be my tour guide for two days.

The kind women at Pro Terra Sancta set up this four-day excursion into Samaria. Jesus intentionally walked through Samaria out of obedience to his

Father. I, too, wanted to walk where Jesus walked and where he met the Samaritan woman at the well. Jesus answered her, "If you knew the gift of God and who it is that asks you for a drink, you would have asked him and he would have given you living water (John 4:10, NIV). I visited this well located in the modern-day city of Nablus in the crypt of the Greek Orthodox Church of Jacob's Well. I will share more on this experience shortly.

Iyad and I have become great friends, and I ended my trip to Samaria as a guest at his home in Bethlehem on Pentecost. The drive north was uneventful; filled with olive trees, small farms, sheep, rolling hills with scattered communities and a few checkpoints along the way. It is unnerving to pass through a checkpoint with a guard pointing a fully locked and loaded rifle directly at you. As a veteran of the military with experience pulling guard duty, I could see the angst in many of their faces. The nonverbals spoke loudly, "I do not want to be here. I do not believe in what we are doing here. This is not sustainable."

Now place yourself as a Muslim living in the occupied West Bank. Their daily life including water, electricity, building permits, and commerce is controlled by the Israeli Civil Administration. Their infrastructure pales in comparison to the Israeli communities. Let us call what I witnessed what it is. It is apartheid! The Israelis promote racial segregation and discrimination against the Palestinians socially, politically, and economically. In essence, I witnessed a master-slave society. Apartheid is a crime against humanity and a slow genocide. The root cause of this violent apartheid system of occupation robs Palestinians of freedom, land, and the right of self-determination.

On October 7, 2023, the violence escalated in Israel with a heinous attack launched from Gaza by Hamas that indiscriminately killed Jews, Palestinians, and Christians. All lives matter and escalating the violence is not the answer. I am in full support of defending your homeland and people in a manner that minimizes collateral damage. Hamas is the enemy, not the Palestinians. The Palestinians are an asset and to treat them with dignity and respect will grow unity within the Holy Land. Between the Jews and Palestinians let us adopt the mantra: the best revenge is "no" revenge. There are numerous evil forces on both sides that fuel the fire of hatred instead of fanning the flames of peace and love. So, when the good are unafraid, evil has no stronghold. In Genesis chapter 25:9 (NIV), his (Abraham's) sons Isaac and Ishmael buried him in the cave of Machpelah near Mamre, in the field of Ephron son of Zohar the Hittite. Even brothers Isaac and Ishmael were able to set aside their differences to focus on what united them.

Instead of focusing on the generational traumas and brokenness in families and cultures, God invites us to focus on the generational strength that only comes from God, as God is love. We are all made in God's divine image. Our DNA is love and love is what connects all that is good. All we have to do to fix the world is to love one another. As a Christian, I believe that in all life's problems big or small, the answer is Jesus Christ-simple yet true. When Jesus is all we have, Jesus is all we need!

On October twenty-fifth, 2023, I received a text from Ali, my Muslim friend living in Bethlehem. I made five visits to Bethlehem during my stay in the Holy Land. I witnessed much of what Ali laments: "What is Israel planning? Is this why it delayed the ground incursion? Bombing limited areas today in Jenin and over the past few days in a number of areas in the West Bank…daily incursions into cities and villages, closing roads and cutting off connections between the West Bank and Jerusalem…continuous arrests and restrictions on the prisoners. Two prisoners were martyred, one of whom was twenty-five years old…the settler's seizure of new lands in the West Bank…the complete closure of the Ibrahimi Mosque to Muslims…daily raids on Al-Aqsa Mosque that did not stop throughout the war. Cutting off water to villages and cities in the West Bank for weeks and cutting off electricity whenever they want, for whatever reason. Israel changes the reality in the West Bank and Jerusalem dramatically and is trying to liquidate the West Bank from any form of resistance and make people's lives hell so that they cannot breathe during the attack on Gaza and until it follows the transfer of Gaza to Egypt and deports the people of the West Bank and Jerusalem to Jordan."

My response to Ali: "Greetings brother, All the above is true…God is not pleased with the way Israel is treating the Palestinians and other non-Jews. Judgment will come. Accountability, transparency and justice with compassion will be served. The big question to you and those afflicted is are we willing to forgive and break the generational traumas, curses, and brokenness of the past and replace them with the love of God manifested through the love of neighbor? Unconditional love is the greatest healer. Forgiveness is love in action. Lead with love!" Ali agreed with my response. We all know that love is the answer. God is love and God wins!

During my stay in the Holy Land many Muslims including my friend, Iyad, told me that they have never traveled outside the occupied West Bank their entire life. I felt sympathetic anger as I have come and gone at will during my "Pentecost" in the Holy Land. When the world gives you obstacles,

God gives you courage, resiliency, and the power of prayer. For God has not given us a spirit of fear but of power, love, and self-control (2 Timothy 1:7). "Father God, I praise you for filling me with the Holy Spirit so I can overcome the obstacles and challenges facing me and the world today. Thank you for giving me the courage to accept my mission to encourage reconciliation through love and forgiveness to all families and cultures in accordance with your divine will, all for the Glory of God"!

The Lord granted us safe travels to Sebastia, and we met Majdi at the local park over a cup of tea. Majdi is a middle-aged man with a dynamic personality whose name means "praiseworthy." Sebastia is believed to be one of the oldest continuously inhabited places in the West Bank. In the ninth century BC, it was known as Samaria, and served as the capital city of the northern Kingdom of Israel. Samaria was renamed Sebastia by King Herod the Great in honor of Roman Emperor Augustus as "Sebaste" in Latin translates to Augusta. Today, Sebastia is an all-Muslim community of 4,500 people **(12)**. Majdi informed me that the last Christian died in this community in 2021. He was the caretaker of the local cemetery. I visited the tomb of John the Baptist and the local mosque.

Majdi and I then walked above the town square to visit the ancient Roman ruins that once stood as a colosseum and theater. On our way up the hill, we stopped and gave directions to a young Finnish couple with an infant. They, too, were looking for the way to the ruins. Majdi invited me to sing at the theater at the center of the stage where he explained the acoustics were ideal. I joyfully sang, "Praise him, praise him, praise him in the morning, praise him in the noontime. Praise him, praise him, praise him until the sun goes down." By George, my voice sounded better at the center of the stage or at least that's what I was led to believe. We then visited an olive orchard where I stood beneath a 600-year-old olive tree. The olive harvest occurs throughout the Holy Land in October. Many local and international volunteers assist the farmers in the harvest.

Many locals were gathering for the weekend festivities as well as a few of us tourists. A large Palestinian flag waved proudly in the air. I felt a sense of peace and tranquility there not felt anywhere else in the West Bank. Madji and I enjoyed a fabulous Mediterranean lunch together at the "Holy Land Restaurant" consisting of organic wheat soup, hummus, olives, salad, yogurt, chicken and fresh bread from the open-hearth oven. This concluded my first day in "Samaria." The Mosaic

Guesthouse for the next two nights was in Nisf Jubeil, a community of 400 residents a few kilometers from Sebastia. Nisf means a small mountain and jubeil means half. Together it translates into a village on half of a small mountain.

My guest room was one amongst three rooms located in a courtyard adjacent to the outdoor dining room in a picturesque setting carved into the side of the mountain. The cave room was empty and had a glass floor over a series of caves. It was quite spectacular. The other room was occupied by the young Finnish family. I was blessed to cross their path three times in the same day, indeed a *Godcident*. He is a political science professor at the University of Helsinki in Ramallah. Ramallah is the de facto administrative capital of the state of Palestinian located six miles north of Jerusalem.

Across from my stay was a multi-generation Muslim home with very kind occupants. I quickly made friends with a three-year-old and we warmly greeted each other with hugs. I enjoyed tea and conversation with the family in the evenings. Rami was the caretaker, chief bottle washer, and cook at the Mosaic Guesthouse. This huge man had the heart and smile of a child.

I was cordially invited to join seventeen Sicilians for supper and dancing at the outdoor venue. The evening was spectacular as the courtyard was decorated with multicolored lights, the food was delicious, and the Arabic dancing was my highlight. Three men energetically synchronized their steps to lively and entertaining music that filled the night air. Their joy and exuberance encouraged all of us to partake in the festivities. A blessed day in Samaria!

The following morning Rami was hard at work in the kitchen. This allowed me a few minutes to take a walk through this small hillside village. I met the town donkey. Maybe he was a descendant of the donkey that Jesus rode into Jerusalem? I was invited to sit with Amiel and his son Ahmed outside their country home amongst the flock of sheep. Here I am in the "occupied" West Bank where it is advised that I not travel. The irony of it all is the West Bank is where I found the most peace and harmony. The people were genuine and kind. The people were the "good Samaritans." Kindness matters!

I did not stray too far from the guesthouse as I knew Rami's breakfast would soon be served. And what a feast it was! There was not one item that was processed. All the food was fresh including the hummus, pita bread, olives, thyme, eggs, cheese, and dates. I added a small cup of Arabic coffee for a healthy start to my day! As I was waiting to meet Majdi in Nablus, I was reminded that there are four very important words in life: love, honesty, truth, and respect. Without these in your life, you have nothing. These words will play a significant role in establishing peace in the Holy Land and throughout the world. The best is yet to come...

CHAPTER 11

NABLUS: CHIEF CITY OF SAMARIA

On Saturday, May twenty-seventh, Madji arranged for me to be picked up by Wilade, a taxi driver from Nablus. Madji was born and raised in Nablus and later I will share our candid conversations around his former political activism and his solution to peace in the Holy Land. Nablus is a quick twenty-minute taxi ride from Sebastia. We could see the sprawling city of 200,000 that lied ahead in an enclosed fertile valley and is the market center of a natural oasis that is watered by numerous springs **(13)**. Many groves of olive trees punctuate the scenery enroute. Wilade took the back roads to avoid checkpoints. As an ancient Canaanite town and chief city of Samaria, Nablus translates to “responsible, disciplined, shyness.”

Nablus is renowned as the home of knafeh (a sweet cheese and shredded pastry dessert). Madji took me through the old city of Nablus and we stopped and watched the local vendors make knafeh. It was quite a treat to see them hoist a three-foot pie pan into the air after being flipped over and then smothered with sugar water. This tasty dessert was a welcome treat but not every day, right Madji! Madji likes his desserts, and he has a few extra pounds that he is trying to lose.

Nablus's economy was traditionally based on agricultural trade and handicrafts—most notably, the important and long-established industry of manufacturing soap from olive oil since the 10th century. A type of castile soap, produced only in Nablus and made of three primary ingredients: Virgin olive oil, water, and a sodium compound, 'qilw', this soap was exported across the Arab world and Europe **(14)**. Our visit was to the Albader Soap Factory which employed fifteen people and manufactured 40,000 bars of soap weekly in a very unique process.

Upon entrance to the factory, we walked around hundreds of fifty-five-gallon barrels filled with olive oil. The ingredients are mixed in huge mixers on the ground floor and then hand carried in large buckets upstairs and poured out onto a smooth stone floor like cement to dry. Once dry, string is placed across the surface to guide the cutting process. A sharp metal blade attached to a long wooden handle cuts the soap into 40,000 bars that will produce forty columns of soap. The soap is individually wrapped and ready for sale where two-thirds is exported and one-third kept in the Holy Land. A kind and patient worker guided me on the technique to wrap the soap in paper. It was not as easy as one might think. This entire process takes five days and is repeated each week.

Now on to Jacob's Well in the crypt of the Greek Orthodox Church of Jacob's Well, where Jesus met the Samaritan woman. The well is still active, and I could visualize and hear Jesus' encounter with the Samaritan woman. The story of Jesus and the Samaritan woman is found in the Gospel of John 4:1-42. In the first century, Jesus was walking on his voyage from Judea to Galilee and had to come through Nablus, which at that time was called Sychar. Jesus stopped by this well to rest and was very thirsty.

While he was sitting there, a woman approached the well to get water. At the time, the well was property of the Samaritan people, so he asked her permission to have a drink. It was not appropriate for a lone Samaritan woman to be associating with a Jewish man, so the woman said to him, "How is it that you, a Jew, ask a drink of me, a woman of

Samaria?" They had a short discussion and Jesus concluded, "Everyone who drinks of this water will be thirsty again, but those who drink of the water that I will give them will never be thirsty. The water that I will give will become in them a spring of water gushing up to eternal life."

It is with pleasure that I share the fascinating story of Archimandrite Ioustinos, the guardian of Jacob's well in the West Bank. Since 1980, this eighty-two-year-old Greek Orthodox Priest has lived at the church as the assigned lifelong position of caretaker of Jacob's Well. It serves as a special place for people of Islamic, Jewish, and Orthodox Christian faiths.

He tells his story below in the first person:

> I have been chosen to defend this holy water with my life. The caretaker of the well before me, Philoumenos Hasapis, was a friend. He was murdered with an axe. Many people have tried to kill me, but I am still here. I will care for this well and church as long as God grants me permission to do so.
>
> I was born April 16,1941, on Ikaria, an island in Greece. When I was young, my home was occupied by the German and Italian Axis forces. This made things very hard for

our family and there were not many good moments I remember from my childhood. I have lived in the West Bank most of my life, so the times I have returned to my family's home in Greece, I felt like a stranger.

My father was a respected engineer on our island. Following in his footsteps was the dream my family had for me. When I was eight years old, I met a very old nun. We would speak often about spiritual things. It was from these conversations that I decided I wanted to be a priest in the Greek Orthodox Church. When I made the announcement to join the priesthood, my family and I did not speak for six years.

I came to Palestine in 1960. I served as a priest in Bethlehem, then in Nisf Jubeil. For many years, I have served as overseer for this region. During these years I learned to speak Arabic, English, and picked up a bit of Hebrew. In 1979, I thought I would be chosen to serve as guardian of Jacob's Well, but my friend and contemporary was chosen for this responsibility. On November 29 of that same year, a madman named

Asher Raby came onto the property. He threw a hand grenade into the church. The explosion caused destruction and fire. Philoumenos ran from the church and the madman fell upon him with an axe and murdered him. After this, the killer escaped.

Following the murder, things were very bad for Jacob's Well. The church was locked for three months, and the keys were taken to Jerusalem. I did not want to be the guardian as I was afraid the same thing would happen to me that happened to my friend Philoumenos. One night I had a dream and, in the dream, I saw a vision of myself repairing the church and serving as the guardian for many years. I went to Jerusalem, got the keys, and soon began picking up the pieces.

In 1982, the madman Raby returned again and attacked one of our nuns with an axe. She was terribly injured. He fled but returned soon after, climbed the wall surrounding the church grounds with a ladder, and came in with hand grenades and his killing axe. He came running at me with the axe. I resisted the attack and broke his leg. He was arrested. Raby was 37 years old at the time and lived in Tel-Aviv. He was a heterodox Jewish man who believed our church did not belong on this site. He had also killed several other people throughout Israel (unrelated to our church).

Once Raby was captured, everything was very good for Jacob's Well. We started to clean up the church and make it beautiful again. I built an office and monastery and started to paint murals on the walls. In 1998, I was able to get a building permit from Yasser Arafat, which enabled us to launch a major construction project to rebuild the church structurally.

In 2009, Philoumenos was canonized by the Holy and Sacred Synod of the Patriarchate of Jerusalem and is now a saint. When we exhumed his body. It was still intact. It had not rotted even though he had been dead for almost 30 years. The body still exuded a most beautiful fragrance. From pieces of his corpse, we have created several relics that have been sent to different churches around the world.

I have built my tomb and created a mosaic of myself above it. Should it be my time to die, I am ready. This water that I protect is crystal clear, delicious and sacred. I have seen it perform many miracles in my lifetime. I drink it every day and bless all of the pilgrims who come to this site. Friends who visit me drink the water for good health **(15)**.

I agree with Father Ioustinos, water is life!

Next, we made a visit to St. Luke's Hospital. With Madji's charm and connections, he arranged a tour with Sammy, the Chief Nurse who has worked there for thirty-eight years. Sammy was a soft-spoken man with a warm smile and easy to talk to. St. Luke's is a forty-eight-bed hospital that delivers over 200 babies per month. Men and women inpatient rooms are on separate floors. There is a five bed Intensive Care Unit that had a census of two patients. The Neonatal Intensive Care Unit had one baby whom I prayed over. I met staff on each floor and the attending physician for the inpatient wards. All staff were very professional and kind. I was impressed with their facilities and the care that was provided. Madji showed me the original dedication stone from the old hospital dated 1886 that said, "To the glory of God." This concluded my tour of Nablus with Madji, and I now am blessed with a new friend.

I highly recommend Madji as a tour guide in Samaria. He has extensive knowledge of this region and is pleasant and accommodating. He is well known and respected throughout the city. It was a pleasure to spend time with him and walk in his shoes for a few days. We had a most memorable conversation while sipping fresh lemonade in the park of his childhood. I witnessed with pride a middle-aged man who reminisces fondly of his mother and his daily visits to the park. To this day he visits the park regularly. I will always remember his "I am a Catholic Muslim who needs his holy water." The holy water he is referring to is a beer or glass of wine.

As promised, I will share some powerful insights and wisdom that Madji has been blessed with. In his younger days, he was a political activist and spent many occasions detained in prison. His candor and wisdom were refreshing. He was spot on when he offered his solution to the Arab-Israeli conflict: One country called "The Holy Land" with open borders. This country is for all people. We must be able to sit at the table as equals in truth, honor and respect.

Honor and respect are the highest forms of love. Then, and only, can we come together as brothers and sisters serving God. When kindness and truth meet, justice and peace shall kiss (Psalm 85:10, NIV). Madji can be contacted through WhatsApp 972599846385.

CHAPTER 12

PENTECOST 2023 IN THE WEST BANK

Pentecost is a Christian holiday which takes place on the 50th day (the seventh Sunday) after Easter Sunday. It commemorates the descent of the Holy Spirit upon the Virgin Mary and the Apostles of Jesus Christ while they were in Jerusalem celebrating the Feast of Weeks, as described in the Acts of the Apostles (Acts 2:1–31). Jesus promised his disciples the Holy Spirit, the paraclete, the helper, the advocate, the Spirit of Truth. God's Holy Spirit is the Spirit of Truth and the voice of God. "But when he, the Spirit of truth, comes, he will guide you into all the truth. He will not speak on his own; he will speak only what he hears, and he will tell you what is yet to come" (John 16:13).

It just so happens that the Jewish Holiday Shavuot, which is Hebrew for "weeks," comes seven weeks after Passover and was celebrated May 25-27, 2023. Pentecost is the Greek name for Shavuot and means "fiftieth day." Shavuot celebrates the giving of the Torah to the Israelites at Mount Sinai. The early Christian Church viewed Pentecost as an extension of the Jewish festival of Shavuot. As reflected in Acts 2:1-31, the Apostles and the Virgin Mary were celebrating the festival of Shavuot and were filled with the Holy Spirt. In this way, both holidays celebrate similar themes, the giving of divine knowledge **(16)**.

My 2023 Pentecost was magical, divinely guided by the Holy Spirit. I started my day in Nisf Jubeil with a hearty Mediterranean breakfast reflecting on my two days with Madji and his incredible wisdom. Yes, one country, no borders, live freely, "The Holy Land" makes sense to me. I was taxied into Sebastia where I met Iyad, who was waiting in the town center visiting with the local men. God blessed us with a cooler day, overcast with some sporadic rain. This was a blessing and a welcome relief from the scorching heat of late spring in the Holy Land.

We were off to Taybeh, the only all Christian community of 2,000 residents in the West Bank. Our first stop was at the Most Holy Redeemer Catholic

Church for mass. I invited Iyad to mass; he politely declined. The mass was celebrated in Arabic by two priests, five altar servers, and an award-winning choir. After mass, I met two nuns that run the K-12 school and was invited for coffee and fellowship. The nuns knew Sister Frida from the St. Joseph school in the Old City of Jerusalem. I then enjoyed coffee and conversation with the priests and parishioners. With their favor, I offered them a prayer and blessing.

Next, Iyad drove us to the famous Taybeh Brewery. As we entered, we met a friendly woman exiting in her vehicle. She informed us that they were closed on Sunday. Understandably, we thanked her for her time. She then asked us to wait for a moment as she made a phone call. Minutes later, another vehicle approached with two men dressed in business suits. We were graciously welcomed by the owners, David and Nadim Khoury. Soon, David's wife Maria joined our group and David and his brother politely excused themselves. David is a Palestinian and Maria a Greek who met at Harvard University. Together they also own and manage the Taybeh Winery and Golden Hotel. Taybeh in Arabic means kind or good.

Maria is a prolific writer and we exchanged books. She gifted me *Christina Goes To The Holy Land.* "This spiritually enriched book promotes

Christian heritage and deep roots by instilling the importance of maintaining a Christian presence in the Holy Land, the land of Canaan" **(17)**. Maria holds a Doctor of Education degree and assisted English teachers with learning new methods in education and modern teaching strategies for the classroom. She also spent three years training teachers in new classroom strategies in the Latin Patriarchate Schools throughout Palestine during the Second Intifada, also known as the Al-Aqsa Intifada, which was a major uprising by Palestinians against the Israeli occupation, characterized by a period of heightened violence in the Palestinian territories and Israel between 2000 and 2005. Strategies included role playing and acting out a scene as well as cooperative group learning responding to a reflected question posed or a challenge asked to be solved. She volunteers her time in the Taybeh housing project and education fund **(18)**. She not only gave us a tour of the Brewery, Winery, and Golden Hotel but she kindly extended her time for visits to the St. George's Melkite Catholic Church and St. George's Greek Orthodox Church. The Holy Land is very fond of St. George. Let's find out why!

"St. George is embedded in the history of the Holy Land, and Palestinian Christians in particular have great appreciation for his story and legacy.

There are many churches, schools and institutions in Israel named after the saint, and countless men throughout the Middle East and all-over South America are named after him in one variation or another. But what is he famous for? And what was the business with the dragon all about?

George was actually from Lod, right next to Israel's main airport. He never stepped foot in England. His father was Greek, and his mother came from Lod, or Lydda, in what was then Palestine. He was born in Turkey, but lived and died in third century Palestine, and was buried in Lod after his death on the twenty-third of April, 303 AD. His hometown is mentioned several times in the Bible, and it was in Lod that Peter healed the paralytic in Acts 9.

He served in the Roman army, and as a high-ranking officer he saw the terrible persecution of the early Christians in the late 200s. He took a brave stand against Rome on the matter and protested against the torture of Christians. Eventually, the Roman Emperor Diocletian ordered his death after he refused to deny his faith in Jesus. He refused to make a sacrifice in honor of the pagan gods.

There were no dragons involved, but he stood up to the specters of Roman brutality and the persecution of God's people. The fanciful dragon story was fabricated sometime around the twelfth century, hundreds of years after our very real saint had died. However, what *is* true is that he battled valiantly against monstrous powers of evil and died a heroic martyr's death in the fight" **(19)**.

Iyad and I enjoyed our visit to Sebastia and Taybeh. In fact, he had never been to either community. It gave me great joy to see him experience his "Holy Land" too. We were then off to Jericho and finally returned to Bethlehem to join his family for supper. Jericho is believed to be one of the oldest cities in the world. In the Bible, Jericho is best known as the location of God's faithfulness to the Israelites as on the seventh day with their trumpet blasts and mighty shout, the walls of Jericho came tumbling down. Jericho was the first city conquered by Israel after crossing the Jordan river into the Promised Land. The city is situated in the lower Jordan Valley, just west of the Jordan River and about ten miles northwest of the Dead Sea. It sits in the broadest part of the Jordan plain more than 800 feet below sea level and nearly 3,500 feet below Jerusalem, which was only seventeen miles away. This geographical detail explains why Jesus said in His parable, in Luke 10:30, that the good Samaritan "went down from Jerusalem to Jericho" **(20)**.

We first stopped to quench our thirst and

enjoyed a carrot, ginger, orange "packed full of nutrients" juice. Then, Sammy the camel was calling my name. His master, a very pleasant Bedouin assured me that Sammy was docile, sure and steady. Indeed, Sammy was all of that and more. Sammy gave me a kiss on the side of my face to show his gratitude. I think I might have blushed.

I visited the Zacchaeus tree as described in Luke 19:1-10. Jesus entered Jericho and was passing through. A man was there by the name of Zacchaeus; he was a chief tax collector and was wealthy. He wanted to see who Jesus was, but because he was short, he could not see over the crowd. So, he ran ahead and climbed a sycamore-fig tree to see him, since Jesus was coming that way. When Jesus reached the spot, he looked up and said to him, "Zacchaeus, come down immediately. I must stay at your house today." So, he came down at once and welcomed him gladly. All the people saw this and began to mutter, "He has gone to be the guest of a sinner."

But Zacchaeus stood up and said to the Lord, "Look, Lord! Here and now, I give half of my possessions to the poor, and if I have cheated anybody out of anything, I will pay back four times the amount. Jesus said to him, "Today salvation has come to this house, because this man, too, is a son of Abraham. For the Son of Man came to seek and to save the lost."

We then traveled to the Mount of Temptations (Mount Quruntul) outside of Jericho. "Jesus, full of the Holy Spirit, left the Jordan and was led by the Spirit into the wilderness, where for forty days he was tempted by the devil. He ate nothing during those days, and at the end of them he was hungry" (Luke 4:1-2). On this visit the Greek Orthodox Monastery of the Temptation embedded into the side of Mount Quruntul was closed. I was able to visit this Monastery later as part of my group pilgrimage.

Now, the best was yet to come with food and fellowship. We returned to Bethlehem and stopped at the local butcher shop and bought lamb and beef for Iyad's "best kabobs in Bethlehem." I was privileged to be a guest in his home on the feast of Pentecost. Iyad and his wife, Lemma, have two daughters and one son. While the master chef was preparing the kabobs, I had the opportunity to read a portion of *God Loves the Children* to his children along with a few of their friends. That "holy moment" was priceless.

We enjoyed endless servings of beef and lamb kabobs with peppers, onions, and tomatoes. After supper, we sipped on a cup of sage tea while visiting with Iyad and his father, Calid. It was a wonderful experience to celebrate the feast of Pentecost with my new Muslim family. Many Muslims' extended families live in the same dwelling. It is common that the parents occupy the ground floor, and each family unit builds upon that. Currently Iyad and his family were occupying his brother's floor as he was working abroad. With great pride, Iyad showed me his floor and the plans he has soon to complete his floor for his family. I offered some financial assistance, and my friend wasted no time in making his dream come true. Now enclosed, he is methodically finishing the inside of his "dream home."

Wow, what a Pentecost day! Come Holy Spirit Come! As I departed for the Bethlehem Eman Regency Hotel, I was graced with soft rain and a cool temperature. In the morning, Iyad dropped me off at the bus stop to take bus #231 back to Jerusalem to prepare for my journey into Jordan. Pentecost 2023 in the West Bank will undoubtedly be etched in my memory for years to come. Thanks be to God!

Monday, May 29, was a day of rest and transition. I stayed one night at the Villa Brown Jerusalem Hotel. This hotel was a restored nineteenth century villa with charm and a quiet courtyard. That evening, I volunteered to lector at mass at the Notre Dame Center and then dance with my friends at the St. Louis French Hospital. I went to bed early in anticipation of my early morning wakeup and departure for the Kingdom of Jordan.

CHAPTER 13

WADI RUM AND PETRA, JORDAN

I seldom sleep well the night before an early morning departure. I was eager to travel with Abraham Tours to Wadi Rum (Valley of the Moon) in the Kingdom of Jordan. I was less thrilled about my 2:00 a.m. wakeup call and 3:00 a.m. bus departure from the David Citadel Hotel-a convenient fifteen-minute walk from my hotel. We traveled south through the Negev desert for four hours to Israel's southernmost city of Eilat on the Red Sea. Eilat is a tourist destination with sunny days and warm seas near the Egyptian resort city of Taba and Jordanian resort city of Aqaba. The tourist bus was not made for our comfort. I sure could have used a little more leg room. Nonetheless as the dawn broke, the desert beauty erased any negativity of my physical discomfort. I was traveling to the Kingdom of Jordan!

At the border, we paid our fifty-dollar Visa entrance fee at Aqaba and loaded into our Jordanian tourist bus under the capable care of our charismatic guide, Amet. We spent a few hours in Aqaba along the Red Sea and then made our way to Wadi Rum, which was approximately a one hour's drive. The red rock wilderness accented by a deep blue sky was magnificently beautiful especially at dusk and dawn. "Gargantuan rock formations, rippled sand dunes, and clear night skies create an almost fairy-tale setting across an unpopulated area the size of New York City. This is truly the 'reddest' part of Jordan, colored by iron oxide, and by far the most dramatic in terms of landscape.

Over 20,000 petroglyphs and 20,000 inscriptions have been documented inside Wadi Rum, tracing human existence back some 12,000 years in this spot. Even today, some nomadic Bedouins who are sheep and camel herders make their home here, along one of the migratory courses modern humans took out of Africa, providing a living portrait of our human origins" **(21)**.

Our first order of business was a truck ride through Wadi Rum. Five trucks with six passengers each loaded up in the back of Toyota pickup trucks sitting on padded bench seats in the open air. It was just as one would expect-five trucks racing across the desert floor jockeying for position. We stopped at various scenic overlooks and rock formations. We witnessed a caravan of camels being herded to our camp for evening camel rides. They were much more disciplined in their travels than our jeep drivers, following one another in a single file.

We were treated to tea at a Bedouin gift shop and enjoyed walking in the dry sandy riverbeds and learning about the exploits of Lawrence of Arabia during the Arab revolt against the Ottomans during World War I. Our guide Amat was very spirited, and his prior military service added credibility to our discussions on the geopolitical and military influences that shaped the current Holy Land conflict.

The day ended as we checked into our humble desert villas located in the Rum Magic Village. Our cottages were clean with all the comforts necessary for our desert outdoor experience. Upgrades included dome cottages with star gazing windows. We had a few hours to relax in the village as supper was being prepared.

We watched the chefs pull the lamb and chicken out of the four-foot pit covered with a steel door with a fire of olive wood burnt over a bed of sand. The entrees were loaded on a three-tiered steel cart cooked to perfection over a four-hour period. The delicious entrees were the highlight of the Mediterranean buffet supper. What do you do in the desert after a wonderful meal? In Rum Magic Village you dance Jordanian style! A dozen of us weary travelers locked arms and learned Arabic line dances for a few hours outside under the stars. After an action packed twenty-hour day, I welcomed and appreciated a restful night's sleep.

The following morning, I arose at dawn to watch the sunrise over the red rock landscape as I was treating my mind, body, and spirit to Jesus or "holy yoga." Only in the deserts of Utah in the United States have I seen such spectacular sunrises. Thank you, Creator of heaven and earth! Our group enjoyed a delicious buffet breakfast and then boarded our bus for the two-hour drive to Petra (rock). "The Rose City is a honeycomb of hand-hewn caves, temples, and tombs carved from blushing pink sandstone in the high desert of Jordan some 2,000 years ago. Hidden by time and shifting sand, Petra tells of a lost civilization. Little is known about the Nabateans—a nomadic desert people whose kingdom rose from these cliffs and peaks, and whose incredible wealth grew from the lucrative incense trade route along the King's highway connecting Arabia with Egypt.

The Romans arrived in 63 B.C., signaling a new era of massive expansion and grandiose construction, like the theater that seated more than 6,000 spectators, as well as some of the city's most impressive facades. Carved into the rock face, the Treasury and the Monastery both have unmistakable Hellenistic (Greek cultural) influence, with ornate Corinthian columns. Petra's engineering phenomena are legendary, including the sophisticated water system that supported some 30,000 inhabitants. Carved into the twisted passageway of the Siq, the irrigation channel drops only twelve feet over the course of a mile, while underground cisterns stored runoff to be used in drier times of the year" **(22)**.

Petra was destroyed by an earthquake in 363 AD and was a lost city until it was rediscovered in 1812 by Swiss traveler and geographer, Johannes Burckhardt. We began our hike at the Petra Visitor Center in Wadi Musa (the valley of Moses). This is where Moses struck water from the rock and where the prophet Aaron is buried. During the first part of this trail (950 m), you will walk through the gateway to the Siq or "shaft." The famous and stunning Siq is a 1.2 km corridor 3-12 meters wide with walls reaching as high as 182 meters. It is a natural splitting of the mountain assisted by water erosion. An aqueduct system ran the length of the Siq, collecting seasonal rains that would be stored in multiple cisterns throughout its course.

At the end of the Siq, you will see the magnificent Treasury, also known as Al-Khazneh, as you exit through the narrow canyon. The Treasury was constructed in the first Century BC is forty meters high and intricately decorated with Corinthian columns, friezes, and figures. The Bedouins (nomadic desert dwellers) claimed the treasury concealed the pharaoh's treasure. Also, throughout the trail Djinn blocks or burial monuments with tombs were scattered along the hillside **(23)**.

In front of the Treasury was a large open area for tourists to gather and camel rides and vendors competed for our generosity. Below the winged Lion Temple, I met Ahama, a Bedouin shop owner. I first purchased a freshly squeezed orange juice and then he offered me a cup of black tea with cardamom. He lived in a large cave in the local area free of all utilities and modern-day comfort. He showed me pictures of his expansive dwelling decorated with ornate Arabic rugs. We took a picture together with big smiles and a peace sign to give honor to the Creator and to each other.

For those with mobility challenges or preferred to ride, horses and golf carts were available for a modest price. As a suggestion, I recommend a three-day tour of Wadi Rum and Petra spending an extra day in Petra. One day in Petra was not enough to truly enjoy its beauty and historic sites. In 1985 Petra was declared a United Nations Educational, Scientific and Cultural Organization (UNESCO) World Heritage site. In 2007, Petra was voted one of the new seven wonders of the world. We enjoyed a delicious Mediterranean buffet in Petra before returning to the border at Eilat. We easily cleared through customs and onto our Jerusalem bound bus for our late-night return to Jerusalem. The whirlwind tour of Jordan will be a fond memory for a lifetime.

Upon my return from Jordan, I walked up the hill to my stay at the YMCA Three Arches Hotel for a few nights. The kind receptionist was awaiting my late check in and greeted me with a warm welcome. This unique, interesting and historical building was completed in 1933. It has beautiful public areas with arches and lush gardens as well as complimentary use of the exercise facilities including free zumba, yoga, and spinning classes.

CHAPTER 14

TEACHING IN JERUSALEM

I was up early the next morning, Thursday, June first, to meet my friend Paul Calvert from Bethlehem. Each Thursday he visits a few schools in Jerusalem to spread the gospel message. He invited me along as his guest. We visited the Makor Hatikvah Messianic Hebrew School in Jerusalem with 140 students from first through ninth grade. Paul arranged for me to speak to the ninth-grade students at the school. After a brief tour of the school, I had the distinct pleasure to present the *God Loves the Children book* and the Creator model of healthcare in a very interactive and lively setting to about twenty students. To share the gospel message of salvation through healthcare to Jewish children was certainly one of my highlights during my "Pentecost" in the Holy Land.

Makor Hatikvah means "Source of Hope." Makor

Hatikvah's “vision is to academically, spiritually, and morally equip the current generation of Israeli Messianic children and youth to be a light to our people and take on leadership roles in every area of our society in order to affect the spiritual environment of Israel. Makor Hatikvah's mission is to provide an alternative source of education for the children of Israeli Messianic Jewish families as well as temporary or long-term believing families who desire that their children become an integral part of Israel's society during their formative years; and to provide them with an excellent Hebrew education that is both academic and spiritual, with an emphasis on the shared culture, history and values of our people; to promote a love for God and His Word, to encourage a personal walk with Yeshua, the Messiah of Israel, respect for others and accountability for one's actions; and finally to equip our students for higher education, giving them the foundational skills and values necessary to live their lives as Jewish believers in the land of their forefathers” **(24)**.

Then we were off to the Little Hearts Preschool. This Preschool offers a faith-based Montessori education in Jerusalem. Little Hearts works to make a difference in the lives of children through a loving and nurturing environment that models unity amongst the Arab, Jewish, and international communities. They offer an age-appropriate Montessori curriculum and take care to nurture the whole child: spiritually, emotionally, intellectually, socially and physically **(25)**. We gathered the toddlers and pre-kindergarten students in the play area and sang "May the blessings of the Lord be upon you" and "Talk to Jesus my guiding light." I shared the parable of Jesus healing the paralytic of thirty-eight years and the Good Samaritan. We shortened our program to meet the attention span of our very important little people. Sometimes, less is more.

Then Paul introduced me to Stephanie, the office manager, at the Anglican International School Jerusalem (AISJ). This school offers a safe, happy and caring environment where a deep mutual respect and a love of learning is at the heart of all they do. Their education goes beyond the classroom, permeating the hearts of future doctors, teachers, lawyers and business leaders. The AISJ stays true to its great historical Christian foundations in the knowledge that we are all made in the image of God who created the universe and each individual. "We believe that each child is precious in the sight of God, therefore we are committed to the advancement of education to children from all faiths and none, and every background to promote a culture of respectful coexistence. A school founded on

Christian principles admitting children from forty-five nations from preschool to twelfth grade with staff from Muslim, Jewish and Christian faiths working together in harmony, mutual respect and love" **(26)**.

As I was sharing my love for Jesus Christ, "the perfect Jew", outside of Stephanie's office, I later was informed my exuberance for Jesus was insensitive as our conversation touched the ears of a Jewish employee. In my heart, I made no apologies for sharing my love for Jesus Christ and may this plant a seed for growth. I love and follow the perfect Jew and may my example encourage others to follow. Thank you, Paul, for your love of Jesus Christ and allowing me to join in your ministry for the morning. Now it was time for me to return to the hotel and get caught up on rest, journaling, and finalizing arrangements for my much anticipated trip to Nazareth and the Sea of Galilee.

After a restful and productive afternoon, I attended the evening mass at the Notre Dame Center. It is the holy sacrament of communion, the body and blood of Jesus Christ, which draws me faithfully to daily mass. Partaking in the body and blood of Jesus Christ is my daily miracle. I become what I receive. The Eucharist means "thanksgiving" and is my daily spiritual nourishment. This helps me keep my eyes on the prize, Jesus Christ.

"Amen, amen, I say to you, unless you eat the flesh of the Son of Man and drink his blood, you do not have life within you. Whoever eats my flesh and drinks my blood has eternal life, and I will raise him on the last day. For my flesh is true food, and my blood is true drink...Just as the living Father sent me and I have life because of the Father, so also the one who feeds on me will have life because of me" (John 6:53-57) **(27)**.

After mass, I invited Jacob, "the Jesus guy" to supper on the rooftop terrace at the Notre Dame Center. "Barefoot, dressed in white robes, Carl James Joseph, a Catholic pilgrim from Detroit, Michigan, has been living without money and depending on the generosity of others for the past twenty years. Joseph calls himself Jacob but is better known by many as 'the Jesus guy', a moniker he has earned as a result of his Jesus-like appearance and active choice to live like he believes the Bible figure did more than 2,000 years ago.

He has visited about twenty countries in the world as a missionary and has become a well-known figure in the old city of Jerusalem, where he explores the life and path of Jesus Christ. 'The Jesus guy' does not carry objects or money and walks around the streets of the Old City barefoot, wearing white robes and carrying a woolen blanket and Bible. He spends most of his day praying at the Church of the Holy Sepulcher and talks to people who he meets on his way" **(28)**. Jacob and I enjoyed a delicious meal and a very spiritual conversation before he excused himself to go pray, you guessed it, at the Church of the Holy Sepulcher.

After supper, I walked outside onto the terrace overlooking the city of Jerusalem. This is a spectacular vantage point that I visited a few times during my Holy Land visit. At night, the city becomes alive, and the historical sites in the Old City illuminate in the moonlight. It was here that I met a fellow physician and pilgrim. Allow me to introduce Dr Mark Hickman, a retired thoracic surgeon from New Braunfels, Texas. He currently is performing vasectomy reversals and delights in the opportunity to give couples hope to be "fertile and multiply." We both shared our spiritual journey and expressed our gratitude to God for his grace and mercy. Next, it was time to rest for my journey the next day to Jesus' hometown of Nazareth. *Jesus, we are going to show honor in your hometown all for the glory of God!*

CHAPTER 15

NAZARETH: THE HOMETOWN OF JESUS

I arose early Friday, June second, which starts the Jewish Shabbat. Travel can be restricted from Friday late afternoon to Saturday late afternoon. Therefore, I decided to catch the 8:00 a.m. bus from the central bus station in Jerusalem to Nazareth. There were a few more buses leaving later in the morning, but the early bird gets the worm. I was privy to the schedule as a kind employee at the central bus station gave me a copy of the weekly schedule a few weeks ago when I was arranging my travel to Nazareth.

Despite the fact that the Torah mentions the word "Shabbat" more than eighty times, only a few of these references deal specifically with how one is to observe the Sabbath day. The first reason the

Torah gives begins in the book of Genesis: “On the seventh day, God finished that work that He had been doing…And God blessed the seventh day and declared it holy, because on it God ceased from all the work of creation that He had done” (Genesis 2:2-3). Although there is no mention here that human beings should also observe a Sabbath, in the book of Exodus (in the first articulation of the Ten Commandments), God declares that the Israelites should “remember the Sabbath day and keep it holy…for in six days the Lord made heaven and earth and sea, and all that is in them, and He rested on the seventh day; therefore the Lord blessed the Sabbath day and hallowed it” (Exodus 20:8).

“Together, these passages give us the profound concept of *imitatio dei*—the imitation of God—in association with Shabbat. We should rest because God rested—and we should ‘remember’ Shabbat and keep it holy. We also implicitly learn that even God, as it were, needs a break. And if God, the Creator of the universe, needed to rest (and sanctified that rest), how much the more so do we human beings need a weekly opportunity to cease from all productive activities, from ‘creating.’”

The second reason the Torah gives for observing Shabbat appears in the version of the Ten Commandments presented in the Book of

Deuteronomy. God says, “Remember that you were a slave in the land of Egypt and the Lord your God freed you from there with a mighty hand and an outstretched arm; therefore, the Lord your God has commanded you to observe Shabbat (Deuteronomy 5:15). This explanation touches on two momentous motivations for observing Shabbat. The first is the covenant between God and the Jewish people: God redeemed the Israelites from slavery, and the Israelites must observe God’s commandments. The second motivation suggested by these phrases is one of deep empathy with our enslaved ancestors. Because our forebears who were slaves were unable to enjoy a day of rest, we should observe Shabbat as a demonstration of our own redeemed status–and perhaps, with a consciousness about those who are still enslaved” **(29)**.

The two-hour bus ride to Nazareth went quickly as I was engaged in a conversation with a young man named Boaz. He is now an engineering student after his three-year service in the Israeli Defense Force in communications. Myself, a veteran of the Army and Air Force, we soon became kindred spirits. This polite and helpful young man represented Israel very well. He was meeting his parents short of Nazareth at another bus stop. The landscape was engaging with lush rolling hills brimming with abundant corn, wheat, sorghum, tomato, cucumbers, and peppers grown in irrigated fields.

"Most of Israel's agriculture is based on cooperative principles that evolved in the early twentieth century. Two unique forms of agricultural settlements: The kibbutz, a collective community in which the means of production are communally owned and each member's work benefits all; and the moshav, a farming village where each family maintains its own household and works its own land, while purchasing and marketing are conducted co-operatively. Both communities provide a means not only to realize the dream of the pioneers to have rural communities based on social equality, co-operation and mutual aid, but also to gain agricultural output in a productive means" **(30)**.

"Nazareth is the largest city in the Northern District of Israel. In 2021 its population was 77,925. Known as 'the Arab capital of Israel', Nazareth serves as a cultural, political, religious, economic and commercial center for the Arab citizens of Israel, and became also a center of Arab and Palestinian nationalism. The inhabitants are predominantly Arab citizens of Israel, of whom 69% are Muslim and 30.9% Christian. Nazareth is home to the largest Arab Christian community in Israel and the Christian communities of Nazareth are varied and include various denominations. The most prominent among them are the Greek Orthodox, Melkite Greek Catholic, Latin Catholics, Maronites, Armenian Orthodox, and Protestant. The city also commands immense religious significance, deriving from its status as the hometown of Jesus, the central figure of Christianity" **(31)**.

The Casa Nova provided my lodging during my stay in Nazareth. It was only a three-minute walk from the bus station and directly across from the Basilica of the Annunciation. This Franciscan place of hospitality was well maintained with spacious rooms, delicious meals, a chapel nestled in an underground cave, and service with a smile. I met sister Wilina from Cebu, Philippines in the chapel. She was a great resource and very helpful during my stay. She invited me to mass at the chapel for the Saturday evening mass. She was delighted that I was a lector and asked me to read at this mass. I spent four nights at this hospitality house for pilgrims in the hometown of Jesus Christ. I was thrilled!

After I was settled into my room, I made final arrangements to meet with Bishop Riah Abu El-Assal. Bishop Riah's name was given to me by Maria Khoury while I was in Taybeh. She felt that Bishop Riah would be very helpful in my ministry. Bishop Riah is the former Anglican Bishop in Jerusalem. During his thirty-two years as a priest in

Nazareth, he actively sought through church, politics and diplomacy for a peaceful resolution of conflict in the Holy Land. He was installed in 1998 as Bishop of the Diocese of Jerusalem and the Middle East **(32)**. Bishop Riah was delighted to meet me and after picking me up at the Casa Nova, we drove a short distance to his office. He showed me the remodeling project throughout the complex and was most proud of his beautiful produce and flower gardens.

With his soft voice and warm smile, Bishop Riah was kind, humble, and inspiring. He shared his journey as a young boy in exile, then returning to his homeland as a servant of God as a priest and Bishop for decades. We enjoyed sharing our ministries and exchanging pictures with gifted books to one another. Bishop Riah was in full support of opening a dialogue in establishing the Jesus of Nazareth International College of Osteopathic Medicine in Nazareth. He continues his ministry seeing hospitalized patients at the Edinburgh Medical Mission Society (EMMS) Hospital in Nazareth.

His book, *Caught in Between—The extraordinary story of an Arab Palestinian Christian Israeli* captivated and motivated my spirit. This book is a roadmap for peace. In his last chapter, "The Good Samaritan", Bishop Riah emphasizes "that the wounded man that was saved and was healed made known that there is good in the world. He told of his suffering, but also of the restoration of hope and that good will ultimately prevail. The Samaritan acted out of conviction that the man was worth the life God had given him. He simply helped heal the man and gave him strength to stand again by himself. When the Palestinian people receive the help they need to stand by themselves again, they will not forget. They will share their experience with others."

The last paragraph of his book ends with: "We have yet to discover who will be our Good Samaritan. We continue to pray for him and like the wounded man we may have to wait for a stranger, someone not of our own, to fill the role" **(33)**. After much prayer and discernment, I texted Bishop Riah, "I am the Good Samaritan." On May 31, 2023, two days prior to our visit, he was awarded the Jerusalem Star by President Abbas of Palestine for his longstanding work for peace, justice, and reconciliation.

After our morning together, Bishop Riah kindly dropped me off at the EMMS hospital for my meeting with the Frank Kantor, the spiritual director. Frank and I met for over an hour discussing the power of love and forgiveness in the healing of the mind, body, and spirit. We both agreed, it is not only the answer to the conflict in the Holy Land, but for humanity. He, too, was intrigued with establishing a medical school in Nazareth that embodied the healing power of love. Jesus came to earth to teach, to love, and to heal. It would be a great honor to Jesus to establish a medical school in Nazareth with His name promoting His ministry.

Frank suggested that I visit the Nazareth Village adjoining the YMCA below the hospital. "Set on the outskirts of Old Nazareth, Nazareth Village is built on ancient agricultural land that boasts the area's only first century wine press. The original farm has been restored with its ancient wine press, terraces, irrigation system and stone quarry, with replicas of first century houses, a synagogue, a watchtower, mikveh (Jewish ritual bath) and olive presses have been carefully constructed using the original building methods and materials. Together, these elements form the Nazareth Village, an authentic first century farm and recreation of the hometown of Jesus with real ties to the life and time of his friends, family, and fellow Nazarenes" **(34)**.

As I entered the YMCA, I took a picture of the engraved sign embedded in the stone: "That youth may grow in wisdom, stature, and favor with God and man." I was greeted warmly by the receptionist and added to a group tour by our guide Nathaniel.

The one-hour tour was educational and enlightening. Our first stop was to watch David thresh the wheat with a rake-like tool separating the grain from the shaft. Then we met Simon, an elderly man, who was busy tending to the cabbage, cucumbers, and melons. I will never forget his ear-to-ear smile and his parting words to us: "I love Jesus more than I love myself." Nathaniel showed us almond, fig, pomegranate, and apple trees on our way to the wine press. The wine press was strategically placed below the grape vineyard. In a flat stone area, the workers would walk barefoot crushing the grapes releasing the seeds and juice to flow down into a small cistern to be placed in goatskin flasks.

The process to make olive oil with the olive press was remarkable. The guide explained that olive berries were put in the press and crushed with a huge millstone. "The first press produces extra virgin olive oil, which is used to light the Jewish temple. The oil from the second press is used for medicine, while the oil from the third or last press is used for making soap. That's what happened to Jesus in Gethsemane. Gethsemane, which means 'oil press', was where Jesus was first pressed in a time of darkness (Luke 22:53), so that we will always be in the light and walk in the light **(35)**.

The second press took place after Jesus was brought from Gethsemane and scourged. Jesus is our 'medicine' because *'by His stripes we are healed'* (Isaiah 53:5). The last press, in which the oil is used for cleansing, happened at the cross. Jesus was crushed under the fiery indignation of a holy righteous God, suffering the judgment and penalties for our sins. His blood has cleansed us of our sins **(36)**. Olive oil in the natural has no effect on you unless you eat or use it. But when you pray over your bottle of natural olive oil in Jesus' name, God sets it apart and it becomes holy anointing oil. Use the oil for God's glory and see His miracles, provision and restoration in your life" **(37)**! Now let's reveal the beauty of the olive tree.

"When you study the olive tree, you will be blessed because every part of the tree has a meaning. When you go to the Garden of Gethsemane in Israel, you will find really old olive trees with gnarled trunks. Interestingly, the trunk of an olive tree is hollow unlike most trees. Why is the olive tree trunk hollow? The olive tree represents each of us and God wants us to remember always that we are created by God with this purpose—to contain Him only, not ourselves or the devil. People who don't fulfill or refuse to accept God's purpose for them will feel empty inside. They can do many things to fill themselves up—live for pleasure, earn lots of money, get whatever they desire—but they will end up feeling empty. You can even see the emptiness if you look really close into their eyes. But when you look at those who are full of God, there is a fire in their eyes and a spring in their step everywhere they go.

In the Bible, God describes His people of Israel as the '*Green Olive Tree'*. (Jeremiah 11:16) We, who were formerly Gentiles, have been grafted into this olive tree. (Romans 11:13–25) The olive tree lives long, so expect to live a good, long life" **(38)**.

Then we were introduced to the herb za'atar. "It can be hard to find this herb and is commonly made from dried thyme, oregano, sumac, and sesame seeds. The recipes vary depending on what region they're from, with each household having their own special blend. Some za'atar recipes also contain salt, marjoram, sumac berries, dried dill, dried orange zest, caraway seeds, or hyssop. Each meal za'atar is served with hummus, olive oil and pita bread" **(39)**.

We watched Hannah weaving wool into blankets and Joseph working diligently in his workshop. Our final stop on the tour was at the Synagogue where Jesus would teach and pray. Nathaniel eloquently recited the Sermon on the Mount at the bimah, or podium, in the center of the sanctuary. Then I walked back to the Casa Nova and enjoyed a refreshing beet, carrot, and ginger juice made with perfection by Amman. I would visit his juice stand daily during my stay in Nazareth. Wow, my first day in Nazareth was blessed and the best is yet to come!

Allow me to digress here to share a prayer that was answered by God while I was visiting my brother and his family in Guatemala in March of 2023. As I was planning my seven-week Pentecost, I left plenty of room for the Holy Spirit to work. My calendar started to fill in with excursions to Jordan, the Sea of Galilee and throughout the West Bank. Then after a few days in prayer, I felt the Holy Spirit direct my thoughts to Nazareth. My excitement grew as I was determined to give honor to Jesus in his hometown. The following day, I departed for home and as we followed a bus to the airport there was a huge sign in the back window in capital letters: NAZARETH. With a broad smile and a look up to heaven, I said, "That was you Jesus!" Prayer is our lifeline and Jesus is our anchor. When prayer becomes your habit, miracles become your lifestyle.

On Saturday, June third, I attended the morning mass at St. Joseph's Church in Arabic. During my stay in the Holy Land, I would attend mass most days in either Italian, English, Spanish, Arabic, or Hebrew. The beauty of the mass is the liturgy is the same in all languages and the prize is the Eucharist, the body and blood of Jesus Christ. The Eucharist is the miracle that is witnessed each time mass is celebrated. After mass at St. Joseph's, I toured the underground caves at St. Joseph's Church, visited the Greek Orthodox Church, the Anglican Church where Bishop Riah was a priest, the White Mosque and the Synagogue Church in the Old City, and the Basilica of the Annunciation. It was at the grotto chapel at the Basilica of the Annunciation that I was asked by Sister Wilina to be the lector at mass, reading out of the book of Tobit where Tobias took great care to bury the dead at his own personal risk. The mass was live streamed on EWTN (Eternal World Television Network). You must be present to win—a reward of attending daily mass. You may watch the entire mass at this link:

https://www.youtube.com/live/pVVs2LIW-DY?feature=share

The rest of my day was filled with visiting vendors and picking up a few souvenirs while enjoying walking the streets where Jesus grew up. The Arab people were very kind and friendly. I enjoyed learning about their culture and cuisine. I was becoming proficient at saying thank you (shukran) and you are welcome (afwan). Those simple yet very important words brought smiles and genuine appreciation into our conversation. I learned that the large grape leaves that were sold in the market were for making Warak Dawali, which was stuffed grape leaves with ground sheep, spices, and rice. This is very similar to our cabbage rolls or stuffed peppers.

At the Basilica of the Annunciation, I met Fady, a Catholic Arab who was very helpful in arranging visits with his physician cousin, Kamal and the Bishop of Nazareth, Rafic Nahra. Both pledged support for the Jesus of Nazareth International College of Osteopathic Medicine. Also, I became friends with the owners of the Reeja Gallery, Café, and Bed and Breakfast, Samer and Areej. I was fascinated and impressed by how Areej uses olive oil and candle drippings in many of her pieces of artwork. I also met Samer's sister and brother-in-law Souad and Amir and I would return to Nazareth the following week for three days to share *God Loves the Children* at the Sisters of St. Joseph Catholic School and a private venue at the Reeja Gallery and Café. Souad is an Arabic teacher at the Catholic School, and she was instrumental in obtaining approval for my presentation and arranging for the venue at the gallery and café. You can follow Areej on Facebook at Reeja gallery and café.

Outside of the Basilica of the Annunciation, I met Jairus selling olive wood rosaries. I purchased a few of the rosaries for my souvenir collection. Biblically, Jairus was a synagogue leader whose twelve-year-old daughter was raised by Jesus from the dead.

Here, I also met a street man named Josiah whose name means "God supports and heals." He had a large stage three ulcer on his left lower extremity almost to the bone. It did not appear infected as he walked with a pronounced limp. He asked for money to buy food. Then, Jesus and I invited him to eat shawarma and falafel. He graciously accepted and after our meal was completed, he thanked me and limped away. I would see Josiah a few more times outside of the Basilica during my stay in Nazareth. I left Nazareth on June sixth for Haifa and the Sea of Galilee and would return on June eleventh through the thirteenth.

CHAPTER 16

HAIFA AND AKKO

I took bus #331 from Nazareth to Haifa. The one-hour ride traversed through fertile valleys with luscious produce throughout. Haifa is Israel's third largest city after Jerusalem and Tel Aviv. After arriving at the bus station, I found the taxi stand and seventy shekels (eighteen dollars) later, I was taxied to my hotel. I left my travel arrangements for the next two days in the capable hands of the Holy Spirit. Guided by the kindness of Juliana at the Haifa Tower Hotel, she connected me with Kobi, an established and highly recommended guide. An hour later, Kobi picked me up at the hotel and we were off exploring Haifa. Kobi told me that Haifa comes from the Hebrew words "hof yafe" meaning beautiful shores. Indeed, Haifa is a beautiful city nestled between the shores of the Mediterranean Sea and Mount Carmel. Kobi is Jewish and informs me that Haifa prides itself on religious and ethnic tolerance. In fact, our last stop of the day was a visit to his Muslim friend, Mia, at the Mahmood Mosque.

But first, Kobi made me a wreath of Daphne (laurel) worn as a crown on my Jerusalem cowboy hat. Newly crowned, we proceeded to the top of the Baha'i Gardens in awe of their nineteen manicured terraces with lush trees, flowers, and bushes. According to Kobi, the numbers nine and nineteen represent completeness and spiritual growth and expansion respectively. From our vantage point, Kobi pointed out the German colony community beyond the Baha'i Dome Temple with the Mediterranean Sea in the distance. Later in the day, we completed the Baha'i Garden tour viewing this magnificent site from below. You can enter the Baha'i Garden and walk up the nineteen terraces. This is time-consuming and not much is gained at the expense of other attractions.

Next, we visited Elijah's cave in Stella Maris (Star of the Sea) in the Basilica of Our Lady of Mount Carmel. This is where Elijah hid in the cave to avoid persecution waiting on the voice of the Lord. He did not hear the Lord's voice in the wind, earthquake, or fire, only in the quiet whisper (1 Kings 19:11-13). Tourism is hard work, so it was time for some street food in Wadi Nisnas (Valley of the Mongoose), a very quiet and inviting Muslim community. We were treated with samples of all types of Mediterranean food including falafel, shawarma, and delicious desserts.

Kobi saved the best for last, our visit with Mia to the largest Mosque in Haifa, the Mahmood Mosque. Mia welcomed us as brothers with tea and crackers. We visited for a half hour about the God of Abraham and our desire for peace and love. We prayed together inside the Mosque and met others along the way. Kobi took a picture of the Jew, the Muslim, and the Christian smiling and praying together in a Mosque worshipping the one and only God! I will also remember Kobi's comment: "Be the person that you want to meet." We even watched a few wild or feral hogs rooting for food as we left the mosque. There are signs throughout the city cautioning people about feral hogs. Kobi sees them often throughout his travels. Since Haifa has abundant green spaces and forests, the feral hogs have flourished. They are mainly destructive to property with rare attacks on people. After a full day filled with history, culture, and beautiful sites, I walked to a Romanian restaurant down the hill from my stay. The cabbage and salad appetizers were delicious, whetting my appetite for the succulent lamb kabobs. I retired early for bed to meet Kobi in the morning for another full day of sightseeing and fun in the sun!

Kobi picked me up at 8:30 a.m. and we drove to

Breada's bakery for a cup of coffee and croissant. For a large city, traffic was manageable and flowed smoothly. We ate on a terrace overlooking the Mediterranean Sea blessed with another sunny day. Kobi's game plan for the morning was to take a cable car ride up Mount Carmel to Haifa University and visit the Hecht Museum in the thirty-story university building. Then, we planned to spend the afternoon in Akko or Acre just up the coastline from Haifa. Kobi's experience and intuition were on full display as the events of our day unfolded.

The cable car ride from the central bus station to the top of Mount Carmel and Haifa University is a must do attraction. The cost was five shekels ($1.50) each way and the views up and down were breathtaking. Once at the top of Mount Carmel, you can see all of Haifa and the coastal community of Akko. The view from the thirtieth floor of the university building was most impressive. In the Hecht Museum, which was endowed to always offer free admission, Kobi took a picture of me next to an exhibit that said Physician: Medicus: Teacher. I viewed a ship that was found in the Mediterranean Sea that was dated back 2,700 years and is preserved with polyethylene glycol.

I am glad Kobi's intuition was spot on as the afternoon in Akko or Acre was spectacular. As we entered the Old City, there was a beam stretched between two walls. This is where criminals were hung as a visual reminder to all that entered. Akko means "until now" and is a short drive up the coast from Haifa. It is believed this is where Noah sent the dove that returned with an olive branch. By this, they knew the flood ended "until now" and the water regressed.

Akko is a small city; clean and inviting. This is where Napoleon's Army lost its first battle. They breached the first wall and were caught in the open before breaching the second wall that was not expected. As a Veteran, I appreciated visiting the remnants of the fortress that defended Akko. The fortified walls of the fortress with St. John the Baptist Church in the background made for a beautiful picture. We enjoyed a seafood smorgasbord of shrimp, scallops, and calamari on the terrace overlooking the Mediterranean Sea for a total of 190 shekels or fifty dollars. We became part of a cheering section for a young man jumping off the fortress from about fifty feet, making a big splash into the sea. The sea was a magnificent deep blue with brilliant aqua highlights in the shallow water. As we walked through the Old City of Akko, I was surprised and proud to find Native American dream catchers on display. These are a frequent finding in the rich Native American culture in my community in western South Dakota. These dream catchers are handmade willow hoops with a woven net or web. Often, they are decorated with feathers or beads and hung over a cradle or as protection **(40)**.

This ended my two-day tour with Kobi. The venues were enjoyed with the expertise of a kind and knowledgeable guide at a manageable pace. To me it felt like two friends, spending time together learning from one another. I highly recommend Kobi (WhatsApp 972546288862) as a tour guide for Haifa and Akko. Expect to pay 2,000 shekels or ($500) for a full day with Kobi. He was worth every shekel. Tomorrow, Thursday, June eighth, I caught the bus to Tiberias on the Sea of Galilee for four days.

CHAPTER 17

THE SEA OF GALILEE AND THE GOLAN HEIGHTS

I was up in the morning before the break of day to catch a taxi to the bus terminal at the airport. The benevolent receptionist called a taxi for me. The Lord picked Jacob, a stately Jewish man with a refulgent smile contained within his large well-groomed mustache. He was an information gold mine during our twenty-minute ride to the bus terminal. He reminisced about the 1960s and 1970s when the Jews and Arabs were friends and neighbors. Jacob said we all kept our doors unlocked and it was commonplace for Jews and Arabs to visit each other freely. I sensed a sadness in his voice as he then explained the Islamic wars of the 1970s and 1980s that changed the landscape. Amongst the Jews and Arabs that I met, the reoccurring sentiment is a desire for peace. It is the extremists on both sides that do not reflect the majority opinion in the Holy Land. There is no profit in peace.

On the one-hour bus ride from Haifa to Tiberias, I was enamored by the Carmel Mountains, the large fertile plain and inland Jezreel Valley, also known as the valley of Megiddo, and the highlands of the lower Galilee region. At the Tiberias bus station, I was welcomed and given directions for the nine-minute walk to the Casa Nova Tiberias Home for Pilgrims on the Sea of Galilee. I arrived at 9:30 a.m. and my room was not yet available. Rasdi, one of the twelve consecrated brothers and sisters who are the charm and workforce for the Casa Nova Tiberias, politely escorted me to the dining area. In the hallway was a large sign that read, “I have loved you with an everlasting love” (Jeremiah 31: 3). This brought an instant smile to my face. Our ministry tag line is, “Lead with love as the power of love is God.” This modest yet full kitchen facility was accented by a large terrace that overlooked the Sea of Galilee.

“The Sea of Galilee also is referred to as the Sea of Tiberias, Sea of Ginosar and Lake Kinneret. The name that prevailed and made its way into modern Hebrew is Kinneret which means harp for the shape of the lake. This is the way in which it first appeared in the Bible (Numbers 34:11, Joshua 13:27) where it is actually spelled Kinnerot, which is a plural noun in Hebrew. The State of Israel is not just a biblical modern-day miracle; it also features a number of geographical wonders that are unique worldwide. One of these is the Sea of Galilee, which, at 209 meters below sea level, is the lowest freshwater lake on Earth! The other lowest lake in the world is the Dead Sea, which is a saltwater lake" **(41)**.

It was nice to relax and organize my four days on the Sea of Galilee, made possible by a visitor's guide that was located at the reception desk. My must see and do list included the historic sites of Capernaum, Tabgha and a trip to the Golan Heights. I also planned a bike ride around Lake Kinneret which is thirteen miles long by seven miles wide. The distance around the Lake is approximately fifty miles. I walked over to the bike rental at the Aviv Hotel and was greeted by Roy, a very congenial man. The cost of the bike rental was one hundred shekels or thirty dollars for the entire day. Roy informed me that there was a twenty-six km bike path from Tiberias to Ein Gev which was the southern route traveling west to east. The northern route did not have this luxury and was discouraged by Roy. I was now set to explore the lakeshore via bicycle in a few days.

On my way back from the Aviv Hotel, I stopped at the visitor's center, but they were closed. Then came Rami, my Jewish tour guide for the day. He pulled up in his taxi and offered to take me around the Sea of Galilee, to the Golan Heights, and to view the historic sites. Thank you, Holy Spirit! We negotiated a price of 200 shekels (fifty dollars) per hour as we sped away in his taxi. Rami shared that he was a sixty-seven-year-old father of four children ages fourteen to twenty-eight and he lived in Tiberias.

Our first stop was at Tabgha (The Spring of Seven) and a visit to the Church of the Multiplication of the Loaves and Fish, where Jesus fed the 5,000 multiplying five loaves of bread and two fish. I learned about the biblical significance in Tabgha and the "Evangelical Triangle" of Capernaum, Korazim, and Bethsaida where Jesus laid the foundations of his ministry and performed many miracles. These three towns are uninhabited today, fulfilling the bible prophecy: "Woe to you, Chorazin! Woe to you, Bethsaida! For if the mighty works which were done in you had been done in Tyre and Sidon, they would have repented long ago in sackcloth and ashes" (Mathew 11:21, NKJV).

Our next stop was Capernaum 2.5 km away and the main village where Jesus taught and where he picked five of his disciples: Peter, Andrew, John, Mathew, and James. Jesus performed many miracles: Healed the paralytic lowered through the ceiling of Peter's house and delivered the sermon on the Mount nearby at the Korazim plateau. The landscape of colorful flowers and shrubs along with the plentiful mango, avocado, nectarine, apple and other fruit trees throughout “Galilee” enriched the landscape.

Also in Capernaum, I visited the Greek Orthodox Church of the Holy Apostles. The exterior of this magnificent church was white with multiple magenta domes adorned with crosses displayed against a clear blue sky. On the grounds of the church was a large stone table within a pavilion located on the shore of the Sea of Galilee. At the end of the pavilion was an ornamental door that opened into the Sea of Galilee, where one could envision Jesus in fellowship with his disciples.

“The Golan is known as Bashan in the Bible, referenced in Deuteronomy 4:43, 1 Kings 4:13, Psalm 22:12, and Isaiah 2:13 for example. This is where the half-tribe of Manasseh settled, and Golan is named as a city of refuge in Joshua 21:27 **(42)**. The Golan extends about forty-four miles (seventy-one km) from north to south and about twenty-seven miles (43 km) from east to west at its widest point. It is roughly boat-shaped and has an area of 444 square miles (1,150 square km). The better agricultural land lies in its southern portion; the stony foothills of Mount Hermon in the north, with patches of woodland and scrub, are a stock-raising area. The Israeli portion of the Golan rises to 7,297 feet (2,224 meters) at its extreme northeast point on the Mount Hermon slopes **(43)**. Mount Hermon is Israel's highest mountain, sitting on the highest part of the Golan Heights. Snow-capped in winters, this summit is home to Israel's only ski resort in the winter. Here the Jordan River begins on its journey, flowing south into the Sea of Galilee almost sixty miles away. The dew of Hermon described in Psalm 133 paints a picture of majesty and beauty:

> *Behold, how good and pleasant it is when brothers dwell in unity! It is like the precious oil on the head, running down on the beard, on the beard of Aaron, running down on the collar of his robes! It is like the dew of Hermon, which falls on the mountains of Zion! For there the Lord has commanded the blessing, life forevermore **(44)**.*

On the Syrian border we visited Mount Bental. "Mount Bental is one of Israel's favorite mountain peaks to visit, partly due to the great panoramic views of the Golan and even Syria, but also because Mount Bental was the site of a courageous battle fought during Israel's Yom Kippur war with Syria in 1973 for the Golan. This strategic site on the Syrian border is also known as the Valley of Tears due to the enormous losses on both sides. This mountaintop provides both scenic beauty and a glimpse back at the past—with bunkers open to visitors and easy to traverse. The Syrian border and a United Nations peacekeeping force headquarters are viewed in the distance. Maps help to understand the logistics and geography of the battle as well as strategically positioned self-guided audio tours" **(45).** I positioned myself close to a tour guide during my visit and was rewarded with a plethora of insights shared by his knowledge and expertise. As a veteran, I enjoy learning about military history in hopes that we never have to use violence to resolve conflict again. In the parking lot exiting Mount Bental, Rami and I stopped and visited Ahmed, a very charismatic elderly Druze who was selling cherries and other produce.

Ahmed was from Syria but is now living in the Golan Heights. He explained to us that a Druze is a non-Muslim, non-Christian Arab who believes in God. "The Druze in Israel speak Arabic and identify as Arabs, but they are a community distinct from other Arab Israelis, with their own religion and cultural norms. The Druze see their religion, which broke off from Islam in the 10th century in Egypt, as an interpretation of the three large monotheistic religions–Judaism, Christianity, and Islam–and they regard Moses, Jesus, and Mohammed as prophets. The Druze religion has no set rituals and ceremonies, but eating pork, smoking, and drinking alcohol are forbidden. Druze have a strong belief in reincarnation. Druze religious literature is only accessible to a group of religious initiates called the *uqqal*. The Druze religion is closed to outsiders; they accept no converts.

Today, approximately 800,000 Druze live in Syria, 450,000 in Lebanon, and 120,000 in northern Israel. The Druze people in Israel live in the Carmel region, the Galilee, and the Golan. The Druze in the Carmel and the Galilee are Israeli citizens. Most of the Druze in the Golan are Syrian citizens who hold permanent resident status in Israel" **(46)**. Remember, Ahmed, the elderly charismatic Druze selling cherries and other produce? Yes, I bought two containers of delicious cherries from Ahmed. I could not resist his charm.

Now it was time to return to the Sea of Galilee to complete our travels around the lake with a stop at the Kibbutz Ein Gev Fish Restaurant for supper. The trip was all downhill as we left Mt Bental at 1,165 meters (3,822 feet) to return to Tiberias at 200 meters (656 feet) below sea level, and only forty-five minutes apart. Remember, a kibbutz is an agri-cultural community. This community on the Sea of Galilee is well diversified with produce and live-stock. Rami recommended the St. Peter Fish, the fish that fed the 5,000 in Tabgha. Also known as ti-lapia, this delicious freshwater fish is ubiquitous worldwide. I love eating fish, and Rami's recommendation with the customary Mediterranean side dishes was "just what the doctor ordered." We then completed the loop around the lake returning to Tiberias satiated and satisfied for a blessed day around the Sea of Galilee and Golan Heights. Thanks be to God!

On Friday, June ninth, I started off with a breakfast of champions with green olives, garlic, olive oil, pita bread, cereal, yogurt and pastries. At breakfast, I first met Sisters' Shatha and Laura who are Palestinians working in Ramallah. They knew Sister Frida from the Old City of Jerusalem. We spontaneously decided to call Sister Frida and surprised her with a video chat. She welcomed us and was most appreciative of our kind gesture. Then I met Paige, a theology professor at Mount Saint Mary's Seminary in Emmitsburg, Maryland. She was visiting the Holy Land for a few weeks and discussed plans to visit the Golan Heights, Jesus's baptismal site, and the Sea of Galilee the following day. She rented a car and after sharing my experience with her prearranged agenda, I became her tour guide. For the day, however, my intent was a seaside bike ride from Tiberias to Ein Gev. God blessed me with a cooler, overcast day. It was time to ride!

Roy at the Aviv Hotel ensured my bike was fully

operational. I took it for a test ride and all systems were go. I adjusted my helmet and off I rode for the day. It felt great to ride instead of walk for exercise for a change. The cool morning air and breathtaking scenery kept my head on a swivel. The brilliant colors and fragrance of the flora along my travel were pleasant bonuses. It was surreal that I was biking around the Sea of Galilee. This gave me ample opportunity to "talk to Jesus, my guiding light." The communities around the southern portion of the Sea of Galilee are neatly built preserving the beauty and charm of the landscape. In my opinion, The Sea of Galilee remains void of commercial exploitation. Tiberias is the largest city with a population approaching 50,000 people and appears to pride itself in the preservation of their history and culture. Most of the commerce around the Sea of Galilee is generated by agriculture and tourism.

As I made my way around the lake, I was greeted with intermittent clouds and sunshine. I watched with great interest a storm brewing over the Sea of Galilee from the west. At this point, I was approaching Ein Gev on the eastern shore of the Sea of Galilee enjoying a cool breeze for my efforts. I rode under a canopy of date trees, mesmerized by the endless rows of banana, tangerine, citrus, and avocado trees with luscious grape vineyards.

"Kibbutz Ein Gev, located on the eastern shores

of the Sea of Galilee, is one of the largest and wealthiest kibbutzim in Israel. Ein Gev was established, like many of the kibbutzim around the Sea of Galilee, in the mid-1930s as a tower and stockade settlement, with the threat of attack from the surrounding area strong. Today, the kibbutz has a large agricultural and tourism industry. Kibbutz Ein Gev runs a thirty-minute train tour through the Kibbutz, providing an introduction into the unique kibbutz way of life. The route passes through the school, communal dining room, farms and housing areas. Along the journey passengers can descend from the train at the entrance to the banana groves. Here they can learn how bananas are cultivated on the kibbutz and taste the fresh fruit cut straight from the trees. The kibbutz counts tourism as one of its largest industries—operating a holiday resort, one of the largest in the Sea of Galilee area, which opens onto the lake itself with many activities including watersports, and kids' activities such as visiting the dairy farm, banana plantations, and ostrich breeding area." The Kibbutz also runs a fish restaurant where I ate a delicious order of St. Peter's Fish the day prior **(47).** I entered Kibbutz Ein Gev and passed the dairy farm and followed the signs to the boat dock. There I located a lone shade tree along the shore with a fabulous view to consume a banana and a pita jelly sandwich for lunch compliments of my breakfast leftovers. Water with nutritious food is a great welcome combination during an all-day bike ride.

I kept a watchful eye on the storm over the sea as rain fell to the ground a few miles away with sporadic thunder and no lightning. It looked like rain was inevitable for my return trip to Tiberias; fortunately, there were places for shelter enroute. I encountered only a few other bike riders and walkers during my twenty-six km ride to Ein Gev. I certainly was appreciative of the cooler weather and surmised that I would not melt in the rain, so off I went. Within thirty minutes mother nature was kind enough to start with light rain, giving me ample opportunity to find cover under an awning in a campground. From here, I was protected from the rain shower that lasted for twenty minutes. I mused with a smile on how the campers, undaunted, continued to play volleyball, as others were laughing with beverages in their hands. I guess that was me a few years ago. They did not melt, and water is life! The rain shower gifted us with a refreshing coolness to the air. After thirty minutes, the clouds dissipated enough to allow the sun to break through. God's grace was in full swing as I could not ask for a more perfect day to ride in this hot and dry climate.

In my two months in the Holy Land, I witnessed

rain only a few times. Now, the Sea of Galilee was calling me for a swim at a public beach that I passed on my way to Ein Gev. The beach was nestled into a small bay with ample shade and room for activities for the fifty people present. I changed into my swimsuit and with child-like enthusiasm headed into the refreshing water. The Sea of Galilee was surprisingly cooler than I imagined. I floated and swam for ten minutes and then rested under the shade for another ten minutes. I thought to myself with delight, "I just swam in the Sea of Galilee where Jesus walked on water."

There was no sense in changing out of my bathing suit as my next stop was at the Yardenit Baptismal Site on the Jordan. "Yardenit in Hebrew means 'little Jordan River' and is one of the two baptismal sites that pilgrims flock to annually. The other is the Jordan River baptismal site of Jesus (Qasr al-Yahud) near Jericho. Some historians believe that Qasr al-Yahud is also the site where the Israelites crossed the Jordan River to enter the Promised Land" **(48)**. I immersed myself discreetly in the Yardenit away from the crowd and renewed my baptismal promises with Jesus, twice in two days. I would do the same at the Qasr al-Yahud site with my fellow pilgrims weeks later. The Yardenit site was much more commercialized than the modest site at Qasr al-Yahud.

There was no sense in changing clothes for the last hour of my fifty-two km bike ride, so I air dried enroute to Tiberias. I arrived spiritually and physically refreshed and renewed to Tiberias, negating any physical discomfort. The seven-hour excursion was one of the highlights of my time in Galilee. The day was spent in God's creation with fresh air, amazing scenery, visiting historic sites all under the watchful eye and companionship of Jesus Christ. I returned to the Casa Nova to rest and rehydrate prior to supper out on the town.

Within a short walk of the hotel, I was recruited by a spirited waiter at the Galei Gil restaurant to dine on their Lavrac sea bass special. Fish was on my menu, and it did not take any more convincing. I was seated under an awning on the boardwalk overlooking the tranquil waters of the Sea of Galilee. Promptly, I was served eggplant salad with cabbage, pickles, olives and tahini. These are all appetizers that my palate craves and then the baked Mediterranean Sea bass with potatoes soon followed. This was one of the best entrees that I had eaten in a long time. I savored each bite of this tasty meal and all that was left was a pile of bones and two fisheyes looking at me. I strolled up and down the boardwalk as dusk ensued relishing in the blessings of Almighty God! Then, I prayed to the Lord to bless me with a good night's sleep.

Ask and you shall receive, as I was blessed with a restful night's sleep. After another nutritious breakfast, we packed some peanut butter and jelly sandwiches made from breakfast pita. We augmented our meal with some fruit and Paige and I were off to explore the Golan Heights and the Sea of Galilee. My rule on a road trip is to travel with snacks. As the tour guide and navigator, my recommendation was to make a big loop within the Golan Heights extending to the Syrian border. Paige agreed and we soon found ourselves in lush, irrigated farmlands with many small communities and kibbutzim. We first stopped at the Hermon Stream Nature Reserve below Hermon Mountain and walked a half mile along the Hermon Stream shaded by a large canopy of trees. The water is fifteen degrees Celsius or sixty degrees Fahrenheit and is plenteous in aquatic life. This riparian jewel complete with an incredible waterfall is one of Israel's 400 Nature Reserves and eighty-one National Parks. We then made our way to Mount Bental and the Valley of Tears. I enjoyed my second visit to this historic site as I was able once again to visit with Ahmed and buy two more containers of delicious cherries. He must be privy to my road trip rule of traveling with snacks. I gleaned additional information from eavesdropping on a tour guide's conversation and walking through the bunkers and fortifications.

Our next stop was the Druze village of Majdal Shams or "Tower of the Sun" on the Syrian Border. "The drive to Majdal Shams, the center of Druze life in the Golan Heights, is aesthetically spectacular. An expansive town on the rolling southern foothills of Mount Hermon, the view from Majdal Shams is full of green: Apple and cherry orchards; expansive vineyards; Israeli army outposts; and grazing sheep" **(49)**. Majdal Shams sits at an elevation of 1,151 meters or 3,777 feet above sea level.

At Mount Bental, Ahmed explained to us that the Druze are non-Christian, non-Muslim Arabs predominately living in Syria and Lebanon with a minority population in Israel due to the annexation of the Golan Heights. They are a peaceful people who believe in the unity of God as monotheists and do not gather in a church but in homes of fellow worshippers. This community of believers is closed to outside attendance.

This was a great opportunity to stretch our legs and eat our snacks. I strolled through town and visited with a few young Druze men while I was in line for my customary daily "juice." These young men were polite, friendly and highly educated. They professed their love for God and for spiritual purity. Our sack lunch filled our physical needs while our conversations with the people filled our spiritual and relationship needs. The great Lakota Nation has a saying, “Mitakuye Oyasin” which means we are all related; and indeed, we are! We are all one in Christ Jesus (Galatians 3:28).

It was then time to leave the beauty of the mountainous Golan Heights and return to the Sea of Galilee at 200 meters (656 feet) below sea level and visit the Yardenit Baptismal Site on the Jordan River. We would descend over 1,341 meters (4,400 feet) in an hour engaged in conversation centered on our travel intermixed with theology and world events. I was not shy to jump back into the water and reaffirm my baptismal vows and proclaim my fidelity to Jesus Christ.

Our day was then complete, and we finished the loop back to Tiberias with high and grateful spirits. Paige was an excellent travel companion, and I was blessed to share this day with her all for the glory of God. The following day my travel plans included Megiddo, Mount Tabor, and the Church of the Transfiguration and Paige was traveling to Jerusalem. I ate supper at an Arabic restaurant on the boardwalk and ordered sea bass with a carrot salad in olive oil and sesame. Life does not get much better than this.

As I was walking back to the Casa Nova, I met

a dozen United States Jewish college students attending school in Jerusalem. They were on a weekend holiday from their studies and enjoying the Sea of Galilee. With respect to each faith, we had a spirited "peace and love" conversation that concluded with agreement that the solution to the Israeli-Palestinian conflict is LOVE: "All we need to fix the world is to LOVE one another." Lead with LOVE! I guess life just got better.

On Sunday, June eleventh, I woke up early to honor my mind, body, and spirit with sunrise "Jesus Yoga" on the bow of a sailboat on the boardwalk. The sun was low on the horizon casting its warms rays and copper hues on the tranquil Sea of Galilee. This was also the location the preceding evening that God brought the college students to me for our "peace and love" holy moment conversation. As I was finishing up my meditative exercise, I watched two young fishermen on the boardwalk with hopeful cats at their feet and with a smile, I was thinking, "someday fishers of men."

Feeling refreshed and renewed, it was now time to celebrate the Feast of Corpus Christi in the charismatic Church of St. Peter. This quaint church is embedded within the grounds of the Casa Nova. It is the Holy Spirit filled brothers and sisters led by their young Slovenian priest along with visiting pilgrims that gives this holy place its energy and power. Each person is warmly greeted as they walk into the church and hospitality is the name of the game. At the entrance of the church are statues of Jesus and Peter with three sheep: “Feed my sheep.”

On the Feast of Corpus Christi (Body of Christ), five priests celebrated mass (three Italian, one Polish, and one Slovenian) with roof-raising music praising Jesus, rivaling a Pentecostal revival. Etched in my memory will be the five priests standing behind the altar waving their arms accented by huge smiles for the glory of God. The pleasing harmony of all in attendance reverberated throughout the small spirit-filled church. After mass, we all gathered around the altar for a group picture giddy with love wondering how many Jews in Tiberias were converted with our roof-raising chorus of praise.

After breakfast it was time to check out and meet Rami for my trip to Mount Tabor, Megiddo and Nazareth. The cost for three nights including breakfast was $250 US dollars. Cash was the only form of payment accepted either in dollars, shekels, or euros. I highly recommend the Casa Nova Hotel for its charm, location, price, and opportunity to meet pilgrims from all over the world.

Website | www.saintpeterstiberias.org

WhatsApp | 97246712281

You will not be disappointed.

CHAPTER 18

MOUNT TABOR, MEGIDDO AND RETURN TO NAZARETH

Rami was punctual at 10:00 a.m. and on this clear and sunny day we headed up out of Tiberias to Shibbi, the Arab town at the base of Mount Tabor, and the Church of the Transfiguration. We climbed steadily through Shibbi negotiating the switchbacks along our traverse. Large tour buses must shuttle their passengers with smaller buses to make the ascent to the top. As we ascended, Rami pointed out in the distance Cana, Nazareth, and the Jezreel Valley. At the top, there was a one hundred-meter walk to the picturesque grounds of the Church of the Transfiguration under the watchful care of the Franciscans, who also occupy a monastery adjacent to the church. The white stone multistory church both outside and inside contained multiple small chapels off the main chapel. A sublime fresco portraying the Transfiguration with Jesus, Moses, and Elijah in their glory with Peter, James, and John at their feet is painted over the altar. Every Thursday as I pray the luminous mysteries of the Holy Rosary, it takes me back with a humble gratitude for this experience that God blessed me with.

We descended the switchbacks and make our way to the fifteen-acre Megiddo National Park, an important international trade route city that linked the ancient world powers, Egypt and Mesopotamia. He who ruled Megiddo controlled the trade routes to the Jezreel Valley and the Via Maris (Way to the Sea). The kings came, they fought, they fought the kings of Canaan, in Taanach by the waters of Megiddo; they took no gain of money (Judges 5:19). Revelation 16:16 identifies Megiddo as Armageddon where the great battle of the end times takes place between the powers of good and evil. I envisioned Jesus's triumphant return as our Savior King as I am riding with him! God wins!

"Megiddo was one of the strongest and most important cities of Canaan with abundant springs and fertile valleys. The archeological mound of this important city sits on a vista overlooking the fertile Jezreel Valley. The remains of the palaces, temples, gates, and the sophisticated water system of the city are evidence of its great power" **(50)**. The elaborate tunnel and water system was housed 186 steps deep inside a cave. I walked each step, amazed at this ancient technology. I did not witness any active springs or water flow during my time in this adequately lit underground cavern. This archeological site was declared a National Park in 1966 and UNESCO World Heritage Site in 2005.

From Megiddo to Nazareth was a thirty-minute drive. Rami dropped me door side at the Reeja Café and Gallery for my three-night bed and breakfast stay. I highly recommend Rami's taxi service for your travel needs in and around Tiberias and Galilee (WhatsApp 972505435324). After settling into my terrace suite, Souad and Amir generously invited me to supper. My delicious entrée was Arabic pasta noodles with yogurt, garlic, and tahini sauce with abundant middle eastern spices. For dessert, we all shared a large portion of gelato.

Our conversation centered around my *God Loves the Children* presentation at the St. Joseph Catholic School in the morning, as well as introducing the Jesus of Nazareth International College of Osteopathic Medicine to the medical community. We also discussed the socio-political dynamics in the Holy Land and unanimously agreed that the current path is unsustainable for a peaceful resolution. Souad is an Arabic teacher at the Sisters of St. Joseph Catholic School and Amir works in real estate. As we ended our enjoyable evening, I gifted them a copy of my *All for the Glory of God* daily inspirations and then they kindly returned me to the bed and breakfast.

During my fifty-day Pentecost in the Holy Land, I was blessed to attend mass most days, either morning or evening as my travel permitted. At each mass, I was grateful to receive the miracle of the Eucharist—the body of Jesus Christ. June twelfth was Jesus's special gift to me. It was an opportunity for me to give honor to his hometown where he received little. The day started out with mass at the Basilica of the Annunciation at 6:30 a.m. I quickly visited with Sister Wilina from the Casa Nova in Nazareth. Samer, owner of the bed and breakfast, served me a hearty breakfast with enough for my supper. The gourmet breakfast included a fresh breakfast pizza with vegetables and cheese and sides of cucumbers, tomatoes, hummus, olives, and fermented cabbage. At breakfast, I met Odeh, a friend of Samer, who kindly offered to give me a tour of Nazareth the next morning. With his jolly smile and love for Jesus Christ, I savored this opportunity.

Souad picked me up punctually at 10:00 a.m. and we arrived shortly thereafter at the school. The campus was nestled within a lush green space on a hillside. I was privileged to visit the different K-12 schools with an impressive enrollment of 1,200 students. My presentation was to the seventh and eighth grade students. Prior to my presentation, Souad introduced me to the middle school teachers, and I was able to share a glimpse of *God Loves the Children* and the Creator model of healthcare. I was impressed to learn that all students learn Arabic, Hebrew, English, and French. I was welcomed by all with open arms and felt the power of the Holy Spirit.

On our way to the classroom, I was impressed with their "I am" statements written on the stairs to the second floor. Examples included, "I am blessed to be here. I have a dream. I believe in myself. I never give up. I am prepared to succeed. I am amazing." This was a perfect opening exercise with the seventh and eighth grade students who greeted me warmly albeit bashfully. After my introduction proclaiming, "This must be the 'Crazy for Christ' seventh and eighth grade students," I sang to them, "When I see you smile the whole world stops and stares for a while, you are amazing just the way you are," by Bruno Mars. This proved to be a fruitful ice breaker.

Then we started off with the prayer and unity circle where I taught them that we are all equal and made in the divine image of Jesus Christ. We are all Jesus in disguise. Then came my "I am" statements.

"I am a son of the Most High Jesus Christ. I am claiming my inheritance as made in the divine image of God." After our prayer and unity circle and "I am" declarations, I taught them "brain yoga." This simple and effective grounding or centering exercise starts with our forearms crossed right over left and our thumb and index finger softly pinching our earlobes. With smiles on our faces, we then performed ten deep knee bends. In unison, we proclaimed, "Inhale Love" as we descended and with "Exhale Gratitude," as we ascended and finished the repetition with "Focus on Jesus." We switched our forearms to left over right and repeated ten more times. As one could imagine with a group of teenagers, smiles, giggles, and laughs were plentiful and most appreciated. I reminded the students, "Let your smile change the world, do not let the world change your smile."

After our spirit-filled warmup, we proceeded to one of my favorite grounding exercises. Grounding or centering exercises are quick and effective mental and physical exercises to manage stress, anxiety, and negative emotions in order to focus on the present moment. We entertained ourselves with three rounds of head, shoulders, knees, and toes in English, Spanish, and Arabic. The students were very patient and supportive of me on the Arabic round.

We reviewed keeping our "eyes on the prize" as the path to salvation through Jesus Christ. The students were quick to agree that a relationship with Jesus Christ is our path to salvation. I then reviewed the Creator model of healthcare five pillars of wellness as a guide to empower us to live fully alive in mind, body, and spirit, all for the glory of God. This model of healthcare is free and assists us in staying on the path to salvation as disciplined disciples. The five pillars include:

1. Water is life
2. Food is medicine
3. Exercise thirty minutes daily
4. Sleep seven to nine hours nightly
5. Love and forgiveness for self and others

This bright and lively group of students interacted throughout as we emphasized the "Great Commandment"—to love God above all and to love each other as God loves as the only solution to the complex situation in the Holy Land. All we need to fix the world is to love one another. We sang "Talk to Jesus my guiding light" together and raised the roof of the classroom. I savored each minute of the hour that I spent with the students. I closed with a prayer and sang a blessing over the students and teachers, "May the blessing of the Lord be upon you, we bless you in the name of the Lord."

As we departed the school, Souad introduced me to Sister Manar, the principal, and Osama, a computer teacher. I thanked Sister Manar for the honor and privilege to address her students and staff and gifted her a copy of *All for the Glory of God* daily inspirations. Thank you, Lord, for this opportunity to give honor to you in your native land. I was and still am on cloud nine.

I woke up the following morning refreshed and revitalized after my "day in school." Once again, Samer fed me his exquisite cuisine for breakfast and supper. My tour guide, Odeh, joined us for breakfast and then we walked a short distance to Mary's Well in the Greek Orthodox Church of the Annunciation. This church and the Basilica of the Annunciation are the two claimants to the site of the "Annunciation" where Archangel Gabriel appeared to the Virgin Mary. Odeh sings in the choir at this church and his deep love for Jesus Christ was apparent throughout our time together. We viewed Mary's Well, a close-up view of the altar, with appreciation of the Blessed Sacrament (Eucharist), and a twenty-gallon brass baptismal font. My favorite portrait was God showing approval to Archangel Gabriel's Annunciation to the Virgin Mary, with a picture of a small baby Jesus inside her womb. With his infectious smile and friendly personality, we soon became kindred spirits.

His knowledge of the underground tunnels and caves in Nazareth that run 1.5 km from Mary's Well to the Basilica of the Annunciation was fascinating. Odeh arranged access to the ancient holy caves through his volunteer work close by at the Greek Orthodox Metropointe of Nazareth. The engineers of ancient civilization have my utmost respect for their clandestine ability to build safe havens in the most austere environment to avoid Roman oppression. We weaved through a short segment of the caves with admiration for the skill and determination required to complete such a project.

Next, Odeh showed me the Basilica of Jesus the Adolescent with its gothic-style architecture. This magnificent Salesian church of St. Don Bosco sits high on top a hill overlooking Nazareth. St. Don Bosco is the founder of the Salesian order and renowned for his work in educating and rehabilitating poor and disadvantaged youth **(51)**. As a people person, I enjoy meeting others with the same kindred spirit. Odeh introduced me to Hany at the Synagogue Church where Jesus taught in the Old City of Nazareth. Hany was also a kindred spirit. He spoke with love and authority as his spirit brought life to the stone and mortar of the Synagogue Church with the portrait of Jesus preaching to his disciples.

We passed the site in the Old City, where Hasti

and I *Godcidently* met again from our initial encounter a few weeks prior, two-hours away in Ein-Karem. I winked with a smile and looked up to heaven, and said, "Thank you, that was you God." Our last stop for the day was at Mount Precipice, a steep hill on the outskirts of Nazareth overlooking the Jezreel Valley. This is where the people of Nazareth attempted to throw Jesus off the hillside for his claim to be the Messiah. An engraved stone at the site quotes Luke 4:29-30: "They got up, drove him out of the town, and took him to the brow of the hill on which the town was built, in order to throw him down the cliff. But he walked right through the crowd and went on his way." I could just hear Jesus, "Out of my way, it is not my time!" This ended my tour with Odeh who I also recommend highly. Odeh's WhatsApp number is 972523242119. Then, I was off to rest and prepare my presentation on *God Loves the Children* and the Creator model of healthcare for my new friends and family at the Reeja Gallery and Café.

My kind hosts arranged a quaint terrace gathering and the Lord provided a gorgeous evening full of the Holy Spirit. The audience ranged from adolescents to senior citizens, all expressing an interest in *God Loves the Children* and the Creator model of healthcare. We all have a divine anointing, a mantle to build the kingdom of

God on earth as it is in heaven. God has anointed me to bring to the world the Creator model of healthcare five pillars of wellness. Truly it is divine and a blessing to know God's will for me on earth as it will be in heaven. We deepened our discussion to a proposal to bring the Jesus of Nazareth International College of Osteopathic Medicine to Nazareth. I sensed a growing youthful enthusiasm and excitement amongst the attendees. Dr Nakhle, a seasoned local Internal Medicine physician, was particularly intrigued with this proposal. Plans to bring a medical school to the northern Galilee region have been discussed in the past without firm commitment to move forward. "When the time is right declares the Lord, I will make it happen" (Isaiah 60:22). The seeds were planted and now it is time for the Holy Spirit to grow this prophecy. "For no prophecy ever came through human will; but rather human beings moved by the Holy Spirit spoke under the influence of God" (2 Peter 20-21). It felt extra special spreading the gospel message of salvation in Nazareth. Thank you, Jesus!

The next morning, June fourteenth, I attended mass at St. Joseph's Church adjacent to the Basilica of the Annunciation, ate breakfast, and Samer drove me to the bus station. My stay was a phenomenal experience. Expect to be treated and welcomed as family. Here is the link to their Airbnb:

Reeja art gallery, Nazareth—Updated 2023 Prices (booking.com).

CHAPTER 19

TEAM LOVE GOD ARRIVES AND OLD CITY VISIT

The two-hour bus ride back to Jerusalem afforded me ample time to reflect and reminisce over my forty-two-day solo experience in the Holy Land. I never was alone, I always walked holding the hand of Jesus. Now, I was excited to welcome my Team Love God colleagues: Khai and Ayn with their mothers Elvie and Car. Our yearlong sabbatical spreading the gospel message of salvation through healthcare would fittingly culminate in the Holy Land. How cool is that! Like clockwork, the ladies arrived at the Ben Gurion International Airport on time and boarded the thirty-minute train to Jerusalem arriving at 2:45 p.m. This allowed us an opportunity to enjoy two days together before the start of our group pilgrimage. Thank you, Jesus, for the guardian angels providing safe travel for my sisters in Christ.

I met my colleagues and their mothers with a big smile and hugs as they exited from the train station. They reciprocated and we were off to the light rail a short distance away. Train, light rail within Jerusalem, and bus transportation are all very efficient and inexpensive throughout the Holy Land. It was a quick light rail or tram ride to the "City Center" our point of exit. Our lodging at the Dar Mamilla Guesthouse was a convenient all downhill walk with our roller bags in tow. The ladies rested and refreshed themselves for a few hours after their twelve-hour flight from the Philippines as I finished up some laundry.

Revitalized and eager to explore Jerusalem, we walked along the light rail tracks to one of my favorite street vendors for fresh carrot, apple, ginger, and orange juice. We all ordered one of these health tonics and sat outside under the shade of a table umbrella. The temperature in June in Jerusalem can exceed thirty degrees Celsius or ninety degrees Fahrenheit. This day was quite warm, and the shade offered us a reprieve from the late afternoon sun. This was the first time that I met Ayn and her mother Car in person. Ayn has been a trusted member of Dr George J. Holistic Health and Healing and Team Love God for six years. Khai was instrumental in our successful launch in 2016 as we celebrated this momentous occasion in the Philippines surrounded by her family. We all enjoyed our health tonics as we reminisced about our ministry proclaiming, "the best is yet to come." Now it was supper time and off we went to break bread together.

The food choices are incredible in Jerusalem, and we were swayed to dine at "The Gent." We decided to eat family style with orders of beef kabobs with mashed and baked potatoes and chicken schnitzel. Of course, we started our meal with the standard and nutritious appetizers of salad, hummus, and tahini. Our first "Team Love God" family meal was a huge success and a befitting end to our first day together in the Holy Land.

The next morning, we gathered leisurely for breakfast. The Dar Mamilla is strategically located and a five-minute walk to the New and Jaffa Gates of the Old City. The stay includes a spacious kitchen and dining room that accommodates up to twenty guests (darmamilla@proterrasancta.org). Remarkably, the ladies showed no sign of jet lag as the Lord blessed them with a restful sleep. As we enjoyed our eggs, toast, yogurt, and coffee, we organized our day. The ladies were eager to visit the Church of the Holy Sepulcher also known as the Basilica of the Resurrection. God always brings people together for his glory.

As we entered the Old City through the New Gate, we followed the signs to the Church of the Holy Sepulcher. At times, the signage can be confusing, and I am not bashful to ask for directions. A priest was walking our way and warmly introduced himself as Father Anastasis from Texas. After the introductions were completed, he pointed the way to our destination. Walking through the Old City of Jerusalem is like walking through a maze. In the network of cobble stone streets comes a labyrinth of alleys that resemble the arms of an octopus in a city of only 0.35 square miles with almost 40,000 people. Back on course, we soon arrived mid-morning at the Church of the Holy Sepulcher. I acted as a quasi-tour guide as I made many prior visits to this historic site. We visited and prayed at Golgotha or Calvery where Jesus was hung on the cross. Next to Golgotha was the agony of the Virgin Mary's tribute to her son and a powerful reminder of her love and fidelity. Similarly, we offered praise and glory to God at the Stone of the Anointing and at the site of his tomb contained within a small shrine. Inside the shrine is a small candle lit anteroom. From there, four people at a time enter a small opening into the tomb of Jesus. Inside is a large floral arrangement with pictures of the resurrected Christ. Each group has fifteen to twenty seconds for adoration.

Ayn then asked, "Where is the resurrection represented?" As mentioned in Chapter 3, Google confirmed the answer given to us earlier by the Holy Spirit inspired meeting with Father Anastasis. Attached to the western side of the courtyard within the Church of the Holy Sepulcher was a semicircular dome structure, the "Anastasis", or Resurrection Rotunda. In the center of the rotunda was the tomb of Christ, contained within a small shrine **(52)**. We gave another wink to God as he provided the answer unbeknownst to us through Father "Anastasis." Thank you, Jesus, for your signal of grace. We serve a powerful and "resurrected" Savior!

Prior to leaving the Church of the Holy Sepulcher, Team Love God gifted a few books to fellow pilgrims sharing the gospel message of salvation all for the glory of God. Next on our agenda, we decided to tour the Tower of David Citadel Museum a short distance away. We stopped enroute to "open air" shop and conversed with a few vendors and admired the beautiful flowers, shrubs, and trees. We spent four hours engrossed with interactive videos, movies, indoor and outdoor exhibits with phenomenal views of the Old City and Jerusalem. The "Tower of David" is the remnants of the fortress built by Herod the Great and is located just inside the Jaffa Gate. Sitting high above the fortress is a minaret or lighthouse built by the Ottoman empire in the sixteenth century.

Tourism is hard work, and we fed our ravenous appetites with shawarma and falafel to satiety. While on vacation one must always leave room for dessert. We spied a Golda's ice cream shop enroute back to the Dar Mamilla guesthouse. As we sat down with our "gelato," Italian for ice cream, we sang along to our delight with an elderly Jewish Orthodox man playing "Sultans of Swing" by Dire Straits and "Hotel California" by the Eagles on his electric guitar. This talented musician captivated the bustling crowd much to the delight of Golda's and other merchants. He was most deserving of a monetary tip and a tip of my Jerusalem cowboy hat, so he received both with a big smile and thank you. I was able to attend the 6:30 p.m. daily mass at the Notre Dame Center and was the lector. Part of the reading including the verse out of Psalm 85:10: "When kindness and truth meet, justice and peace shall kiss." This ended the first full day for Team Love God in the Holy Land. Indeed, the best is yet to come...

Friday, June sixteenth was a transition day for Team Love God. Jerusalem is the spiritual center for Jews, Muslims, and Christians. At our guesthouse we met fellow pilgrims from Indonesia, Africa, Europe, and the United States. Team Love

God gifted books to Geoffrey, a cancer prevention researcher from Kenya, a family from Indonesia and to our beloved Eisha, a Muslim, who ensured our stay at the Dar Mamilla was comfortable and enjoyable. We decided in the morning to roll our luggage to our new hotel at the Notre Dame Center about two hundred meters up the street. The receptionist was quite kind and accommodating in holding our luggage until our rooms became available in the late afternoon. Our intuition was "spot on" as we beat the afternoon heat and fatigue of the day's activities.

While at the Notre Dame Center, I introduced Team Love God to Jacob, "The Jesus guy." He mentioned it was his birthday, so we serenaded him with "happy birthday" and with "may the blessings of the Lord be upon you." This act of kindness spawned generous participation from others in the hotel lobby. Kindness matters and Jacob was all smiles. Happy birthday to "The Jesus guy!"

Our next stop was to visit Sister Frida at the St. Joseph Catholic School on St. George's Street in the Old City. A few weeks prior, Sister Frida was so kind to allow me to speak to all her students about *God Loves the Children*. It was during my time with the students that the Holy Spirit inspired me to teach them a new dance alternating feet chanting: "Sa-laam, Shalom, Peace." We took Sister to lunch at the Versavee (Savior's Way) Restaurant across the street from the school. This was Sister Frida's first meal at this restaurant, which came as a surprise to me. She mentioned that they eat exclusively in the privacy of their cloistered community. The restaurant owner and staff immediately recognized her and rolled out the red carpet. A few of the servers were former students of hers at the school and it was nice to see the reciprocal respect given. We enjoyed the soup, salads, and delicious fish entrees. Food and fellowship go hand in hand. I smiled when one of the servers gave Sister Frida a hug as we departed the restaurant. I reminded my colleagues that we should give and receive three hugs daily for the optimal health of our mind, body, and spirit.

After lunch, Sister Frida invited Team Love God for a tour of the school. The school was spacious with large classrooms fitted with the latest technology to accommodate 240 students. The center courtyard allowed for sporting activities with a playground tucked in a shaded corner. Sister Frida was embarrassed with the disrepair of the playground turf. There were many holes and irregularities within the turf that were potential hazards for the rambunctious students.

She mentioned the administration was looking for financial contributions to replace the turf. That's when the Holy Spirit encouraged Team Love God to step up for the children. Six weeks later, Sister Frida messaged us the pictures of the new green and grape colored playground turf with a plaque that said, "God loves a cheerful giver" (2 Corinthians 9:7). A month later, Sister Frida sent more pictures with smiling children enjoying the playground and a "Thank you." On this day, my smile was that of a child. I responded with "God loves the children. May the blessing of the Lord be upon all at the school for a peaceful and prosperous year. The play area looks beautiful."

After our tour of the school, Sister Frida invited us for tea, coffee, biscuits and more conversation. As Sister Frida walked us out of the school, we felt privileged to sing her a blessing of "May the blessings of the Lord be upon you. We bless you in the name of the Lord. May the blessings of the Lord be upon you. We bless you in the name of the Lord!" Sister smiled and blushed and was a most pleasant hostess and now a sister in Christ. As we left, Sister Frida was a recipient of one of my daily "hugs."

Then, I sensed the ladies were ready for some Old City shopping and I had just the place to go. A short walk from the school, we found Old City George's souvenir shop loaded with rosaries, magnets, nativity scenes, t-shirts, crosses, and crucifixes with the bonus of personalizing the merchandise with an engraver. Have you ever met a George that you did not like? I have not. Old City George was the most charismatic, professional and honest salesman that I experienced in the Holy Land. He captivated my four friends for over ninety minutes. He meticulously personalized each piece of memorabilia with his engraver. By the end of our visit with Old City George, there was sweat dripping from his forehead. The ladies informed me later that before our pilgrimage ended, they returned to Old City George for more merchandise.

I gently pried the ladies away from Old City George's souvenir shop, and we made our way through the Muslim quarter to exit the Damascus gate. In my opinion, this gate has the most character and allows for larger gatherings due to its small amphitheater extending out from the gate. "The Damascus Gate is located on the northern side of the Old City, towards the middle of the wall that historically surrounded it. Its location in East Jerusalem, officially makes it a Palestinian site that is occupied militarily by Israel. Walking through the gate takes you into the heart of the historic city, a maze of souvenir shops, eateries, and cafes. The gate gets its Arabic name Bab al-Amoud from the pillar—featuring a statue of Emperor Hadrian—that stood at the center of its courtyard during the Roman-Byzantine era. The name Damascus Gate refers to its role as the point of exit for those traveling to the Syrian capital before the establishment of Israel" (**53**).

We entered the Garden Tomb after a short walk from the Damascus Gate. Some historians believe that biblically this is where Jesus Christ was crucified, buried, and resurrected. "At the place where Jesus was crucified, there was a garden and, in the garden, a new tomb in which no one had ever been laid" (John 19:41, NLT). Upon arrival we were warmly greeted by the host and provided a welcome pamphlet. "Near the Damascus Gate and standing in the shadow of Skull Hill you will find this beautiful garden with its ancient empty tomb. Since 1894, the focus of their ministry has been proclaiming the death, burial, and resurrection of Jesus Christ to the nations, so all can know and live for the glory of Jesus. This is a place of worship, witness, and contemplation. Many come with an organized group; while others come on their own to experience the peace, beauty, and message of this Christian site. Entrance is free. The Garden is a place where faith in the crucified and risen Lord is renewed or begun and lives transformed.

In order to preserve and maintain this special site, the grounds of the garden were purchased in 1894 by The Garden Tomb (Jerusalem) Association, a Charitable Trust based in the United Kingdom. The association is comprised of people from many different denominational and national backgrounds, united by the glorious message of the death, burial, and resurrection of Jesus Christ. The site is maintained by volunteers that come from around the globe and join a team of local Palestinians and Israelis.

For over 120 years, the Garden Tomb has shared the story of the Messiah's crucifixion and resurrection with countless visitors from across the globe. Some believe that this garden is the setting of those gospel events. However, the question as to whether this is the same tomb in which the Messiah was buried is ultimately unimportant. What is important is that visitors to this garden have an encounter with the living Messiah today. This is our prayer and ministry" **(54)**.

Our timing was perfect as we entered the Garden Tomb without waiting. Unlike the small tomb at the Church of the Holy Sepulcher, this tomb was spacious, empty, and without pictures. On the gray wall was a carmine-colored cross with some extra letters and symbols that were not readable. We walked through the shaded gardens, enjoying the welcome relief from the midday sun. As we made our way out through the souvenir shop, I bought Holy Land place mats for my kitchen table. I noticed a section of children's books and felt the Holy Spirit's prompt to ask the assistant manager if *God Loves the Children* could be displayed. She was filled with the Holy Spirit, and I gifted a book to her family. She supported the idea of adding our book and called over the manager, Maxim Rivkin. At his request, Khai emailed him a brief synopsis of the book with our belief that *God Loves the Children* has the potential to touch the hearts of readers in Israel and beyond. The book shares the gospel message of salvation through healthcare to live fully alive in mind, body, and spirit all for the glory of God!

Maxim was prompt with his reply a few days later, "Thank you for your offer. I will add you to the list of possible suppliers for the children's books. The tender for the books in general and for the children's books in particular is planned for the future, but not the near future. So, we will be in touch when the procurement for the books begins." Wow, thank you Holy Spirit! I was able to attend mass that evening at the Notre Dame Center and sing with the choir. Our group pilgrimage officially started this evening, June sixteenth with supper at the Notre Dame Center. Indeed, may the blessings of the Lord be upon us!

CHAPTER 20

THE FR. SORTINO HOLY LAND PILGRIMAGE BEGINS IN BETHLEHEM!

Team Love God gathered in the Notre Dame Center pilgrim dining area to meet Father Anthony Sortino, Legionaries of Christ (LC), our spiritual director and other members of our forty-person pilgrimage to start our June sixteenth through twenty-fourth pilgrimage. In May of 2022, I was blessed to initially meet and spend time with Father Anthony in Italy for the ordination of Father Tamson. There, Father Sortino invited me and Team Love God on this pilgrimage. This marked Father Anthony's twelfth Holy Land Pilgrimage. He is a seasoned veteran and his love for the Lord was on full display. He invited Father Mathew, a priest from the same religious community in California to experience his first Holy Land pilgrimage. Father Tamson also was invited to witness his first Holy Land pilgrimage. Indeed, we were blessed to travel with three priests. Father Anthony graced us with his presence at supper as we were blessed to meet a steady stream of fellow pilgrims. Many of us pilgrims purchased his book, "*Holy Land Pilgrimage—A Practical Guide and Spiritual Resource to Experience the Holy Land*, a fourth edition and an outstanding resource. This book is a gem, and I am glad that I read it prior to my arrival in the Holy Land, as I hit the ground running. I was privileged to visit some of the same pilgrimage sites during my solo time in the Holy Land and count it a blessing to grow in my knowledge and appreciation of these historic sites under the spiritual direction of Father Anthony and our learned tour guide, Sam Makarios.

"The basic definition of a pilgrimage is a journey made on foot or by other means to a site of particular religious significance. The idea of a pilgrimage has incredible strong foundations in both the Old and New Testaments. The spiritual importance of a pilgrimage is manifested often in physical journeys and trials from Abaham's journey of faith all the way to the missionary journeys of St. Paul. One may go on a pilgrimage to ask God for help needed to live more generously your own Christian vocation once back in your home. Therefore, the pilgrimage is not just a journey to a religious interest. Alone or with others, it is a physical component of the path of one's heart toward God" **(55)**. For me, it was a call to give glory to God by doing His will.

One could feel the excitement in the air as we retired for the evening. Saturday, June seventeenth began our first full day of the pilgrimage through Elite Travel. After gathering for a hearty breakfast, we met our tour guide, Sam Makarios, an Arab Christian living with his family in East Jerusalem. Sam was a very likeable person who combined wit and humor with extensive biblical knowledge to make our experience one to remember. The most important person on our pilgrimage was our bus driver, Rami. He was also an Arab Christian living in East Jerusalem with his family. Rami comes from a family of bus drivers and God blessed him with amazing talent to maneuver the tour bus into some tight spots. Rami was soft spoken with a wide and contagious smile. Rami and Sam have been friends for many decades. Sam and Father Anthony teamed up on a few prior pilgrimages and together we had an all-star trio.

Our first stop was to the Church of the Shepherd's Field in Bethlehem six miles south of Jerusalem. Bethlehem means "house of bread" because of the many wheat fields. The Church is also known as the Sanctuary of Gloria in Excelsis

Deo or Glory to God in the Highest **(56)**. As you enter the grounds of this holy site, a befitting monument of a shepherd and his sheep welcomes you. Inside this historic church, I marveled at the three distinct frescos painted on the walls. "A fresco painting is a work of wall or ceiling art created by applying pigment onto *intonaco*, or a thin layer of plaster. Its title translates to 'fresh' in Italian, as a true fresco's *intonaco* is wet when the paint is applied. The first fresco unveiled the holy family surrounded by shepherds, animals, and angels looking from above. The second fresco reveals the shepherds greeted by the angel of God and the third fresco highlights the shepherds rejoicing with jubilant praise" **(57).**

We attended mass in the small Shepherd's Cave Chapel built under the Church. The small chapel with its smoke-stained black walls was an ideal humble house of worship for our first mass together. It was here that the Shepherds were first greeted by an angel of God announcing the birth of Jesus **(58)**. We were blessed to receive the Eucharist, or the "transubstantiation miracle" at daily mass throughout the pilgrimage. Transubstantiation is the conversion of the bread and wine into the body and blood of Jesus Christ at consecration, with only the appearance of bread and wine remaining. This belief is supported by

Jesus's bread of life sermon in John 6:48-58:

> I am the bread of life. Your fathers ate manna in the desert and they are dead; but this is the bread which comes down from heaven, so that a person may eat it and not die. I am the living bread which has come down from heaven. Anyone who eats this bread will live forever; and the bread that I shall give is my flesh, for the life of the world. Then the Jews started arguing among themselves, How can this man give us his flesh to eat? Jesus replied to them, In all truth I tell you, if you do not eat the flesh of the Son of man and drink his blood, you have no life in you. Anyone who does eat my flesh and drink my blood has eternal life, and I shall raise that person up on the last day. For my flesh is real food and my blood is real drink. Whoever eats my flesh and drinks my blood lives in me and I live in that person. As the living Father sent me and I draw life from the Father, so whoever eats me will also draw life from me. This is the bread which has come down from heaven; it is not like the bread our ancestors ate. They are dead, but anyone who eats this bread will live forever.

Upon leaving the Church of the Shepherd's

Field, I posed for a picture with a young shepherd boy while holding a white unblemished lamb. I was holding the "lamb of God who takes away the sins of the world."

Next, we traveled a short distance to the Church of the Nativity prominently positioned in its magnificence at Manger Square. "The Church of the Nativity of today is chilly and dark, with no pews inside. The original gloss has been restored to wall mosaics that date back to the twelfth century and include saints, angels, and church councils. Inside the church, the entrance to the Nativity Cave is narrow and all enter single file." We eagerly waited in line for an hour to enter the cave. Once inside, the spacious cave was adorned with marble floors, lamps, and mosaics allowing all to mingle as we offered praise and glory to God for his son, Jesus Christ, around the Nativity Grotto. A silver fourteen-pointed star, embedded into the marble floor, marks the traditional site of the birth of Jesus in the grotto underneath Bethlehem's Church of the Nativity **(59)**.

"A short distance south of the Church of the Nativity is a shrine called the Milk Grotto. An irregular grotto hollowed out of soft white rock, the site is sacred to Christian and Muslim pilgrims alike. It is especially frequented by new mothers and women who are trying to conceive. By mixing the soft white chalk with their food, and praying to Our

Lady of the Milk, they believe it will increase the quantity of their milk or enable them to become pregnant. Rows of framed letters and baby pictures sent from around the world to the Milk Grotto testify to the effectiveness of the 'milk powder' and prayer. According to tradition, while Mary and Joseph were fleeing Herod's soldiers on their way to Egypt, they stopped in this cave while Mary nursed Jesus. A drop of Mary's milk fell upon the stone and it turned white" **(60)**.

It was at the Milk Grotto that Cecilia, a fellow pilgrim, lost her balance and stumbled off a platform into a wall, sustaining a large expanding hematoma over her left eye. I was nearby and was on the scene within seconds to assist and evaluate her. I quickly summoned the Great Physician's guidance and heard the voice of the Holy Spirit, "I have got this. She will be fine." Aided by her two daughters and husband, we walked Cecilia to the bus. Out of precaution, we visited the St. Joseph's Hospital emergency department in Jerusalem prior to our departure for Magdala on the Sea of Galilee. Cecilia was seen immediately and remained neurologically stable throughout the afternoon and discharged. I remained with Cecilia throughout the emergency department course, and she remained upbeat and talkative.

The Holy Spirit was true to his words: "I have

got this. She will be fine." Cecilia remained neurologically intact although sporting an impressive hematoma over her left eye. She rested while we monitored her throughout the two-hour bus ride to Magdala. Time healed the hematoma and Cecilia did not miss a beat throughout the remainder of the pilgrimage. This was our only significant medical emergency during our pilgrimage, and we were blessed with the providence and protection of the Holy Spirit. Thanks be to God!

CHAPTER 21

MAGDALA, NAZARETH, CANA, AND MOUNT TABOR

I treasured my return to the Sea of Galilee for a three-night stay at the Magdala Hotel. The hotel is uniquely situated on the archeological site of Magdala on the shores of the Sea of Galilee and Mount Arbel. This is the hometown of Mary Magdalene (Mary of Magdala) who became a loyal follower of Jesus after seven demons were driven out of her by Jesus. Magdala is a unique Holy Land site, a first century city, near Capernaum where the Jewish residents gathered in a synagogue where Jesus visited and taught.

It is home to the beautiful Duc in Altum Church. "Duc in Altum provides a place for prayer, teaching and worship for Christians of all backgrounds and denominations. The building is dedicated to the public life of Jesus, his transforming encounters, and honors the women of the Bible and all women of faith through its Women's Atrium. Duc in Altum draws its name from Luke 5:4 where Jesus instructs Simon Peter, "Launch into the deep" or put out into the deep water. The edifice is composed of six chapels, including the main boat chapel, four smaller lateral mosaic chapels, an atrium dedicated to women as well as the lower-level Encounter Chapel with an impressive mural. Although a building of contemporary design, within it, visitors can find many details connecting the Christian faith to its Judaic roots and ancient Byzantine traditions" **(61)**.

The next day was Father's Day, and I was up early to watch the sun rise over the Sea of Galilee. God provided a beautiful tribute to the dawn of this new day with a brilliant orange sunrise. I strolled to the boardwalk humbled to be walking this holy ground. I warmed up with "holy yoga" stretches and breathing exercises and then went off for a short run basking in the new morning sun.

Team Love God gathered in the dawn of this new day for some group photos as well as promotional photos and videos for our books, *God Loves the Children* and *All for the Glory of God*. The dawn over the Sea of Galilee makes an unbeatable backdrop for photos and videos. Thank you, God, for this opportunity and your blessings. Throughout the pilgrimage we gifted books to our fellow pilgrims and other travelers sharing our gift with the world. All gifts are meant to be shared. After a hearty breakfast complete with raw honey from the comb, in my granola and coffee, we loaded up to visit Cana, Nazareth, and Mt. Tabor.

Our first stop was at the Chapel at the Church of the Wedding Feast in Cana where Jesus performed his first miracle changing water into wine. The married couples renewed their wedding vows in a very heartwarming ceremony. In the basement of the church there is a replica of a stone jar of wine that looks to hold at least thirty gallons. Jesus turned six of these jars of water into wine. Jesus likes a good party! On the top of the glass encasing the stone jar was a wide band of masking tape with many names and positive messages. I added “Lead with Love” as our contribution in creating a culture of love and kindness throughout the world.

A short drive from Cana is Nazareth and the Basilica of the Annunciation. The Basilica has two levels with two separate churches. The upper level is enormous with stunning mosaics of Mary and Infant Jesus donated from many different countries. Here is where Archangel Gabriel appeared to the blessed Virgin Mary and announced that she would give birth to Jesus. The Basilica is built over what

Catholic tradition holds to be the site of the house of the Virgin Mary. The lower level of the Basilica enshrines a sunken grotto that contains the traditional cave-home of the Virgin Mary with a small adjacent chapel. The domed crown on top of the Basilica of the Annunciation symbolizes the blessed mother as the Queen of heaven and earth.

Mass was held in the upper level with Father Mathew presiding and Father Tamson reading the gospel and sharing his inspiring homily on two constants and a variable. It was a special moment to witness our three priests at the altar consecrating the body and blood of Jesus Christ in the Basilica of the Annunciation. We all enjoyed a delicious lunch at “The Holy Land” restaurant a short walk from the Basilica. The appetizer was a tasty orange lentil soup, followed by spaghetti, cabbage salad, roast beef with fried potatoes, and macarons for dessert. As we walked back to our bus, a few of us stopped for a refreshing nutrient packed juice of fresh carrots, apples, ginger, and beets. Indeed, food is medicine! Throughout our pilgrimage we enjoyed five-star service, food, and accommodations.

Our last stop for the day was at Mount Tabor and the Church of the Transfiguration. At the base of Mount Tabor, we reloaded into smaller buses capable of negotiating the tight turns up the mountain. The view from the top was spectacular as we viewed the Jezreel Valley, Cana, and Nazareth out in the distance. It was a delight to revisit this Franciscan site with my fellow pilgrims with Sam's valuable insights. As I mentioned in Chapter eighteen with my first visit to Mount Tabor and the Church of the Transfiguration, this picturesque and iconic setting is under the watchful care of the Franciscans. The white multi-story church both inside and outside contained multiple small side chapels. A sublime fresco portraying the Transfiguration with Jesus, Moses, and Elijah in their glory with Peter, James, and John at their feet is painted over the altar. Every Thursday as I pray the luminous mysteries of the Holy Rosary, it takes me back with humble gratitude that God blessed me abundantly with this sojourn.

As we returned from our action-packed Father's Day, time was scheduled for relaxation and decompression. After supper, all were invited to a "mercy night" of prayer, healing, and deliverance in the downstairs chapel of the Duc in Altum Church. Father Sortino led us in Adoration of the Blessed Sacrament or Eucharistic Adoration. This devotion involves the adoration of Jesus Christ present in the Holy Eucharist, which is the body, blood, soul, and divinity of Jesus under the appearance of bread and wine. Christine Sortino, Father Sortino's sister, and

I paired up as a prayer team. Soft lights and music produced a reverent environment. One by one, fellow pilgrims sat in our presence sharing their heart. We cried, laughed, encouraged, smiled, and prayed with and over our beloved brothers and sisters in Christ. We reminded them to claim their inheritance as sons and daughters of the Most High Jesus Christ. You are so loved!

In many of Jesus's healings he asked the person if they believed in him. Jesus also asked if they believed he could heal them. Jesus knew his authority to heal through his Father and was always moved with compassion prior to healing. Jesus's healing prayers were always short and concise. "Get up, pick up your mat and walk (John 5:8). Go, for your faith has healed you (Mark 10:52). We modeled our prayers for healing and deliverance after Jesus. With hands out palms up, our brothers and sisters indicated that they believed they were worthy of Jesus' healing, and they believed that Jesus would heal them. As healers granted through the power of the Holy Spirit, Christine and I claimed our authority through Jesus Christ and were moved with compassion. "Very truly I tell you, whoever believes in me will do the works I have been doing, and they will do even greater things than these, because I am going to the Father. And I will do whatever you ask in my name, so that the Father may be glorified in the Son. You may ask me for anything in my name, and I will do it" (John 14:12-14, NIV). We believe Jesus!

This "mercy night" was filled with healings on multiple levels. We all felt the power of the Holy Spirit amongst us. Come Holy Spirit Come! This culminated an amazing Father's Day that I will not soon forget. As I laid my head down on my pillow to sleep, I was overcome with love, joy, and overflowing peace. The Lord granted me a restful night's sleep. Thanks be to God!

CHAPTER 22

SEA OF GALILEE: TABGHA, CAPERNAUM, AND THE CHURCH OF THE BEATITUDES

The next morning many of us felt refreshed physically and spiritually and ready to visit the Church of the Primacy of St. Peter Mensa Christi (Table of Christ) and the Church of the Multiplication of the Loaves and Fishes, both in Tabgha, the Church of the Beatitudes, and St. Peter's Church in Capernaum. Pilgrimages require physical, mental, and spiritual stamina. Sleep can be disrupted for many reasons and the agenda is quite full. It is human nature to try to see and do as much as possible in a limited time, but the turtle wins the race. I had many "holy moments" that allowed me to share the Creator model of healthcare five pillars of wellness. We are all responsible for our health and choices. All life and healing come from God. Many times, less is more. Always place God first!

Our first stop was at the Church of the Primacy of St. Peter Mensa Christi. This is the site where Jesus appeared to his disciples after the resurrection and where he gave Peter the keys to the kingdom over the Christian church. "You are Peter and, on this rock, I will build my church and the gates of hell will not prevail against it" (Mathew 16:18). Jesus is declaring that He is the church and Peter is to build Jesus' church. Jesus is the head of the church and we Christians are the body of the church, the body of Christ.

Upon entering this historic site, we welcomed the shade of a tree lined path to the church sitting on the shore of the Sea of Galilee. This small quaint church was built of dark stone and stood proudly on the shore of the Sea of Galilee. Inside, up near the altar was a large irregularly shaped rock named the Mensa Christi (Table of Christ). We all gathered for mass at an outdoor chapel overlooking the Sea of Galilee and the "Feed my Sheep" statue of Peter with Jesus. The venue for this mass was perfect. After mass, many dipped their feet in the cool refreshing waters of the Sea of Galilee or splashed some water on their face or on their head.

Also in Tabgha, we toured the Church of the Multiplication of the Loaves and Fishes where Jesus fed the 5,000, multiplying the five loaves and two fish. On the floor near the altar is this church's best-known mosaic showing a basket of loaves flanked by two Galilee gullet. We watched three talented "artists" restore the fifth century mosaic floor representing the earliest example of a figured mosaic in Palestinian Christian art **(62)**.

Next, we made the short drive up the hill to the Church of the Beatitudes where Jesus gave the Sermon on the Mount. This octagon shaped church sat stately on the hillside where one could envision Jesus preaching to the masses. Surrounding the church is a well-manicured garden of palm trees, flowers, and bushes. The eight sides of this spacious light-filled house of prayer brilliantly display the eight beatitudes or blessings in Latin in the upper windows. The church is Neo-Byzantine in style with a marble veneer casing the lower interior walls and gold mosaic in the dome. Around the altar are mosaic symbols representing Justice, Prudence, Fortitude, Temperance, Faith, Hope, and Charty **(63).**

Our next visit was to Capernaum, the site of

many of Jesus' miracles where He spent many nights at the home of Peter. Jesus worshipped and taught in the synagogue where his teaching made a deep impression on the local people. Unlike the scribes, He taught with authority (Mark 1:21-22). In the same synagogue, Jesus promised the Eucharist in his "I am the bread of life" discourse. "Very truly, I tell you, unless you eat the flesh of the Son of Man and drink his blood, you have no life in you (John 6:22-59). Jesus healed many people of illness or possession by the devil, including Peter's mother-in-law, and raised the daughter of Jarius, the synagogue leader, from the dead. Jesus pronounced a curse on the town, along with Bethsaida and Chorazin because many of its inhabitants refused to believe in Him." To this day, these towns remain only tourist sites.

We walked through the ruins of the partly reconstructed synagogue where Jesus preached and taught. This impressive structure erected in the fourth or fifth century with ornately carved decorations, is the largest synagogue discovered in Israel. Here is where Sam, a biblical scholar and historian, found a shaded area to teach us the history of Capernaum in much the same manner as Jesus taught his disciples two thousand years ago.

Next to the Synagogue is the modern octagon shaped St. Peter's church sitting over the ruins of his home. Under the glass floor, one can see the remnants of a foundation with rooms. I commented that I could get used to attending this church with the gorgeous views in all directions overlooking the Sea of Galilee. I envisioned myself standing at the entrance as a greeter and usher absorbing the magnificence of the moment. After lunch, it was time for our boat ride on the "Uben" and an opportunity to "dance on the water."

As we boarded the boat on a beautiful sunny afternoon, I smiled when I saw the Israeli flag proudly waving in the wind on the large cross displayed at the bow of the boat. Our dynamic first mate introduced us to Jewish dancing first as a group then with partners. This upbeat music energized the faithful and brought smiles and laughter to us all. I enjoyed dancing with my prayer partner, Christine Sortino, to Neil Diamond's classic "Sweet Caroline." Technically, I guess we danced on a boat on the water—the same water that Jesus and Peter walked on. The views in any direction were breathtaking and the hour boat ride most memorable.

We returned to the Magdala hotel and gathered outside at the active Archaeological Park. We spent an hour with Celine Kelly, the site historian, who was able to keep our attention after a long day in the sun as an enthusiastic subject matter expert.

She shared that Magdala's First Century Synagogue is a special jewel in the Galilee region as it is the best-preserved synagogue of the Second Temple period in Galilee. "One of the most significant recent archeological finds in Israel, the Magdala Stone, holds clues that will help scholars establish a more complete picture of first century Judaism. The front of the stone depicts the oldest carved image of the Second Temple's seven-branched menorah ever found and the long sides of stone depict a building with pillared archways" **(64)**. After Celine was finished, it was time for a relaxing swim in the pool. Many other pilgrims and other guests of the hotel also took advantage of this time to enjoy the same. This was our last night in Magdala as the following day's agenda included Stella Maris and the Baha'i Gardens in Haifa, the ruins of King Herod's palace, and theater in Caesarea Maritime with a return to the Notre Dame Center in Jerusalem.

CHAPTER 23

VALLEY OF THE DOVES, HAIFA, CAESAREA MARITIME

June twentieth marked the halfway point in our eight-day pilgrimage as we started our day with a walk in "The Valley of the Doves" or *Wadi Hamam*. "Under the cliffs of Mount Arbel, this valley marks the route of the branch of the old V*ia Maris*, or 'Way of the Sea' that led from the coast inland towards Damascus and eventually to Mesopotamia. Because it passed near Nazareth on its way to the Sea of Galilee, this was doubtlessly the route that Jesus would have taken as he walked from his hometown to the Sea of Galilee, where so much of his mortal mission took place" **(65)**.

Next was a return trip to Haifa and visits to Stella Maris (Star of the Sea) and the Baha'i Gardens.

Mary, one of our pilgrims, led the bus full of enthusiastic believers in the luminous mysteries of the Holy Rosary enroute. A rosary a day keeps the devil away! I enjoyed sharing the experience in Elijah's cave at Stella Maris with my fellow pilgrims followed by mass at an adjacent chapel. Elijah is believed to have prayed at the grotto before challenging the priests of Baal on Mount Carmel as depicted in 1 Kings 18. Our wonderful priests celebrated mass for the faithful in a chapel within the monastery.

Now that our spirit was fed with the body and blood of Jesus Christ, we nourished our bodies with a delicious meal at the Monastery at Stella Maris and delighted in conversation with some of the nuns after our meal. I learned that Our Lady, the Virgin Mary is the "Star of the Sea," a guiding star on the way to Jesus Christ.

Next stop was to the top of the Baha'i Gardens. I could visit these beautiful, terraced gardens each day in awe of the nineteen manicured terraces with lush trees, flowers, and bushes. We took pleasure in many photo opportunities as our panoramic view included the Mediterranean Sea, Mount Carmel, and the breathtaking Baha'i Gardens under a clear blue sky. Sam herded us scattered pilgrims and we were off to the coastal city of Caesarea Maritime to the ruins of King Herod's Palace in Caesarea

National Park. We visited the 3,000-seat outdoor amphitheater and walked along the boardwalk to view the ruins of King Herod's swimming pool and the beachfront arena built for chariot races and gladiators. A portion of King Herod's Palace sitting on a small peninsula was restored and converted into government offices. Today's events placed a punctuation mark on our time in Galilee and the coastal communities of Haifa and Caesarea Maritime. On our return to the Notre Dame Center in Jerusalem, many of us were in quiet reflection on the past few days with an eager anticipation of our visits the next day to the Dead Sea and Jordan River.

CHAPTER 24

BETHANY, JERICHO, DEAD SEA AND JORDAN RIVER

On June 21, 2023, our first stop was in the town of Bethany in the occupied West Bank. Bethany is only two miles from Jerusalem and the hometown of Lazarus, Mary, and Martha. Sam gathered us in the Church of St. Lazarus where we celebrated mass. The gardens around the church provided a sanctuary for quiet prayer and reflection. The raising of Lazarus is a miracle of Jesus recounted in the Gospel of John (John 11:1-44) in which Jesus raises Lazarus of Bethany from the dead four days after his entombment. Outside the church on the façade were pictures of Lazarus flanked by his sisters, Mary and Martha. Just up the hill from this church stood a Mosque and a Greek Orthodox Church making for a very “holy picture.”

Today was the day that we would renew our baptismal sacrament in the Jordan River and take a mud bath and float in the Dead Sea. But first, we were off to Jericho—the lowest city in the world at 200 meters below sea level—and the Mount of Temptations where Jesus was tempted by the devil (Mathew 4:1-11 and Luke 4:1-13). We took a tram ride up to the entrance of the Greek Monastery which is embedded into the Mount of Temptations. This amazing Monastery of the Temptation is still active and riddled with caves and is thought to be built upon the cave where Jesus prayed and fasted for forty days while being tempted by Satan.

The day was heating up and was perfect for a swim in the muddy Jordan River. The color of the water was likened to a cup of coffee with too much creamer. Directly opposite our location on the Jordanian side of the river was an area designated for baptisms as well. For national security reasons, we elected to stay on our side of the river. There was no activity on the Jordanian side except for some friendly soldiers watching with big smiles as we made the plunge for "Jesus." I donned my white baptismal garment and before I was submerged by Fathers Anthony and Tamson, I proclaimed, "Jesus, you are my Lord and Savior," and was totally immersed in the cool water. Many fellow pilgrims joined in on this symbolic act of reverence for our

Lord. Refreshed and renewed, we boarded the bus in our bathing suits to the Dead Sea. We headed for the beach and lathered up with the Dead Sea mud. This mud bath is known to have numerous therapeutic benefits for the skin and chronic pain because of its high content of minerals such as sodium, potassium, and magnesium. I then floated effortlessly on my back enjoying the buoyancy and the soothing effects of my medicinal cleansing.

While enjoying this tranquility, I received a sudden revelation inspired by the Holy Spirit on the solution to the conflict in the Holy Land. The simple answer to this complex problem is love, for God is love. It is your Love God logo. This Love God logo is to become the symbol on the flag of "The Holy Land." God is Love is universally accepted by Judaism, Islam, and Christianity. The Holy Spirit reminded me that this land is for all people. I believe it is through God's chosen people, the Jews, that He expects them to lead with love. To whom much is given, much will be required (Luke 12:48 KJV). There is room for all people that claim the Holy Land. I will devote chapter 30 to this revelation with a call to action for peace. When you ask big things of God, it is a compliment. For the Mighty One has done great things for me, and holy is His name (Luke 1:49, NASB).

CHAPTER 25

THE QUMRAN DEAD SEA SCROLLS

We made a quick stop at the Twins Cave in Qumran to look at the site where the Dead Sea Scrolls were found. Team Love God used this opportunity for group photos while others made their way to explore the Twins Caves. The landscape is arid, barren, and an ideal place to bury these historic scrolls.

> The Dead Sea Scrolls are considered by many to be the most significant archaeological finds of the twentieth century. From 1947 to 1956, thousands of scroll fragments were uncovered from the caves near Qumran, located on the northwestern shore of the Dead Sea. Over the following decades, teams of scholars

pieced these scrolls together to reconstruct an amazing library of texts from the third century BC to the first century AD.

While the Qumran scrolls are the most numerous, hundreds of scroll fragments have been found at several other sites in the Jordan Valley and the Judean Desert. These texts date from the eighth century BC to the seventh century AD and record the life and activities of the people who lived in and passed through these regions. While the scrolls from Qumran are in Hebrew, Aramaic, and Greek, other scrolls are written in Latin, Arabic, and even Nabatean.

The scrolls discovered at Qumran are certainly the best known of the Dead Sea Scrolls, but they are not the only scrolls to have been found. Thus, to know 'What are the Dead Sea Scrolls?' It is necessary to take a wider look. The scrolls cover a wide range of topics and genres. Perhaps the most interesting are the biblical scrolls, which include texts from every book of the Hebrew Bible (Old Testament), with the possible exception of Esther. Other scrolls are Jewish sectarian writings, administrative documents, deeds of sale, and even divorce and marriage records. Despite the name, the majority of the scrolls are preserved as fragments, small scraps of what were once larger scrolls and documents. These were written on various materials, from leather to papyrus. While some scrolls are several feet long, many smaller fragments are no larger than a fingertip. To date, more than 25,000 fragments have been discovered, and extensive work has gone into combining, preserving, translating, and studying these various fragments.

Moving on from the question, 'What are Dead Sea Scrolls?' we now turn to the question of 'Why are the scrolls important?' The discovery of the scrolls is remarkable on several counts. First, it is quite unusual for ancient scrolls, usually written on parchment or papyrus, to be preserved in the archaeological record. The organic nature of such writing materials causes them to decompose rapidly. Yet the arid environment of the Judean Desert allowed these texts to survive. After more than two millennia, they are still legible!

Second, they illuminate the Bible's composition. Prior to their discovery, the earliest surviving copies of the Hebrew Bible dated to around 1,000 AD. The scrolls are a millennium earlier. Scholars are able to see continuity between the scrolls and later biblical manuscripts. Yet they also have found some variation. For example, some scrolls of Exodus and Samuel from Qumran preserve passages that were absent from later biblical manuscripts. These might represent different traditions that were circulating at the time of the writing of the scrolls, or scribal errors that crept into some manuscripts. Thus, the Dead Sea Scrolls are instrumental in reconstructing biblical texts.

Third, they provide a window into the world of their authors. The scrolls did not just rewrite the history of the Hebrew Bible's development; they rewrote the history of Judea in the late Second Temple period. Most of these texts were written when the Second Temple still stood in Jerusalem; when Jewish sects, including the Pharisees and Sadducees, argued about the correct interpretation of the law; and when the Greeks, Hasmoneans, and then Romans, with Herod as a client king, ruled over the region. A few other texts date as far back as the eighth century BC, during the time of the First Temple, while some are as late as the Islamic conquest of the region in the seventh century AD.

Who wrote the Dead Sea Scrolls? Indeed, there is debate about the authors' identities, but many connect them with the Essene community, another Jewish sect, who lived at Qumran. The scrolls, then, would have been their library. As noted above, the environment around Qumran is arid; although it was more fertile in antiquity than today, it still would not have been the most comfortable place to live. Yet it was well suited for the Essenes, who sought to remove themselves from society to live pure, righteous lives in accordance with a strict interpretation of Jewish law. One of the documents uncovered among the scrolls, the *Community Rule*, gives some insight into life for the Qumran community, if indeed they were the authors of the scrolls. We see from other texts that this group was anticipating eschatological events, the end of days. They believed that the promised messiah would soon return, overthrow corrupt society, and usher in the kingdom of God.

The scrolls help us recreate this historical moment. We learn about the varied religious landscape of Judaism during this period—from which emerged early Christianity. For it is during this time, in the first century AD, the final century of the Dead Sea Scrolls' composition, that Jesus of Nazareth launched his ministry. The Qumran settlement was abandoned around 70 AD, about the time of the Temple's destruction, and their library forgotten, that is, until 75 years ago **(66)**.

CHAPTER 26

A FULL, ABUNDANT, AND BLESSED DAY!

June twenty-second marked the seventh day of our pilgrimage and we had a fitting start with mass in the Calvary Chapel at Golgotha in The Church of the Holy Sepulcher, or the Church of the Resurrection, in the Christian quarter of the Old City. We then walked a short distance into the Jewish quarter to experience the Western Wall. "The Western Wall, also known as the 'Wailing Wall' or the 'Kotel', is the most religious site in the world for the Jewish people and is the last remaining outer wall of the ancient Jewish temple, and an incredibly important site of modern Israeli history. Thousands of people of all faiths journey to the wall every year to visit and recite prayers. Traditionally, these prayers are either spoken or written down and placed in the cracks of the wall. The wall splits into two sections, one area for males and the other for females" **(67)**. I had many opportunities to visit and pray at the Western Wall. I placed my prayer requests in the cracks of the wall and made a final visit to the Western Wall on the night before our departure. What I experienced there was miraculous and will be shared in an upcoming chapter. Stay tuned!

I was privileged and welcomed to view a bar mitzvah at the Western Wall. "Bar mitzvah is Hebrew for 'son of commandment.' When a Jewish boy turns thirteen, he has all the rights and obligations of a Jewish adult, including the commandments of the Torah. From that date, he will wear tefillin or a pair of small black leather boxes attached to leather straps containing four sections of Torah on parchment. This milestone is often celebrated with a ceremony in synagogue, tefillin wearing, and parties. The celebrant may be called to the Torah, lead services, deliver a speech or otherwise demonstrate his newfound status. The bar mitzvah is automatic, whether a celebration or special ceremony is held" **(68)**. I observed eight men joyfully singing and dancing with the young man during his coming-of-age ceremony. I offered a silent prayer and blessing for this young man and those participating in his bar mitzvah. Indeed, this was quite an honor!

"For the young women, the bat mitzvah is

Hebrew for 'daughter of commandment.' When a Jewish girl turns twelve, she has all the rights and obligations of a Jewish adult, including the commandments of the Torah. From that date, she takes her place in the Jewish community and celebrates with creative projects, meaningful gatherings, and joyous parties" **(69)**.

I visited with an Israeli Defense Force soldier toting his automatic weapon as I waited for our group to assemble for our short walk to the Dome of the Rock. This would make my third visit to this contentious site during my Holy Land experience. He graciously accepted my request for a picture together and I thanked him for his service from one soldier to another.

"Dome of the Rock, or Mosque of Omar, is the oldest existing Islamic monument. It is located on the Temple Mount, previously the site of the Temple of Jerusalem. The rock over which it is built is sacred to both Muslims and Jews. In Islam, Muhammad is believed to have ascended into heaven from the site. In Judaism it is the site where Abraham prepared to sacrifice his son Isaac at Mount Moriah. Built in 685–91 AD as a place of pilgrimage, the octagonal building has richly decorated walls and a gold-overlaid dome mounted above a circle of piers and columns" **(70)**. Entrance to this site is exclusive to Muslims with rare exceptions and this seventh century monument is an active worship site. I was permitted a brief visit inside the Dome of the Rock and was most impressed with the spacious interior ordained with lavish marble decor and mosaics with Arabic inscriptions.

From the thirty-six-acre campus that houses the Dome of the Rock and Temple Mount we walked through the Lion's Gate in the Muslim Quarter to St. Anne's Church located near the start of the Via Dolorosa (way of the cross). This church is built on the site of the grotto that Crusaders believed was the birthplace of the Virgin Mary and home of her parents Joachim and Anne **(71)**. It is customary that pilgrimage groups offer a worship and praise song in this church to share the love of Christ with each other. When you sing, you pray twice according to St. Augustine. I enjoyed listening to the lively and charismatic Nigerian group that proceeded us as they were on fire for the Holy Spirit! Likewise, our ensemble sang beautifully all for the glory of God!

Team Love God gathered at the Pools of Bethesda to pray over one another. The prayers and blessings that flowed from our mouths inspired by the Holy Spirit captivated our hearts. We recounted the gospel passage from the gospel of John 5:8 where "Jesus said to the paralytic man who had been ill for thirty-eight years, Rise, pick up your mat and walk." I will cherish and remember this moment as a powerful and defining moment for Team Love God.

Yes, today was packed with amazing venues. We then traveled to the Chapel of the Ascension located at the highest point of the Mount of Olives. Following Christ's resurrection, early Christians quickly marked this location. A pilgrim named Egeria found two footprints in a rock in 348 AD, which she claimed to be Christ's before His ascension into heaven. This small chapel was next to the Church of the Pater Noster (Lord's Prayer), a part of the Sanctuary of the Eleona within the Carmelite Monastery where Jesus was thought to have taught his disciples the Lord's prayer. All throughout this historic site, colorful mosaics of the Lord's prayer were displayed in 140 different languages **(72)**. Here, Team Love God beautifully sang the Lord's prayer in Filipino for all to enjoy.

Sam kept us all motivated throughout the day and our last stop was at the outdoor Israel Museum. Here, Sam explained in detail the scale models of the Temple Mount with the Holy of Holies in the center as well as life in Jerusalem during the Second Temple Period. The Holy of Holies is the inner sanctuary of the Tabernacle where God's presence appeared **(73)**. This outdoor gem was a fitting end to a full and blessed day.

The following day was Friday, June twenty-third, and our last full day in the Holy Land. I give my highest recommendation for Sam Makarios as a Holy Land tour guide. Safety is his highest priority and combined with his biblical knowledge, he masterfully parceled out historical information in a manner that was easy to comprehend and absorb. HOME | sammakarios | WhatsApp | 972546496628

CHAPTER 27

GARDEN OF GETHSEMANE, THE UPPER ROOM, AND CHURCH OF THE VISITATION

We started Friday morning by hitting the ground "walking solemnly." We made our way to the Via Dolorosa (the way of suffering) and Church of the Flagellation. The fourteen stations along the Via Dolorosa mark Jesus' path of suffering forced by the Roman soldiers on the way to His crucifixion. Today there are nine stations outside in the streets and the remaining five stations are located inside the Church of the Holy Sepulcher. Station fourteen is where Jesus is placed in the tomb. Team Love God carried the cross as we sang "Behold, behold, the foot of the cross, on which is hung my salvation." This somber experience was soon turned to joy as we proclaimed the glory of the risen Jesus Christ.

Our pilgrimage then took us to the top of the Mount of Olives where we viewed the holy city of Jerusalem. Some pilgrims received an even more elevated view from the top of a camel. Onward to the Church of Dominus Flevit on the Mount of Olives hillside near the Garden of Gethsemane. Dominus Flevit in Latin means "the Lord wept" **(74)**. In Luke 19:41 ESV, we read, "and when he drew near and saw the city, he wept." Through the small western facing window in the church, we had a bird's eye view of the Old City of Jerusalem. At the base of the Mount of Olives we walked through the Garden of Gethsemane reflecting and meditating on the night Jesus was handed over to the Romans by Judas Iscariot. The same night Jesus was praying and sweating blood, His disciples could not stay awake. The agony in the garden is the first sorrowful mystery of the Holy Rosary. The sorrowful mysteries are recited on Tuesdays and Fridays in the Roman Catholic Church. I prayed the Holy Rosary while sitting in the Garden of Gethsemane during my sojourn in the Holy Land. Mass was celebrated inside the Church of All Nations or Basilica of the Agony adjacent to the Garden of Gethsemane. This Basilica was adorned with a beautiful façade of two deer facing one another as described in Psalm 42:1: As a deer longs for a stream of cool water, so I long for you, O God.

We then were transported to the Church of St. Peter Gallanticu located on the eastern slope of Mount Zion just outside of the Old City. On its roof rises a golden rooster atop a black cross recalling Christ's prophesy that Peter would deny Him three times "before the cock crows." Galli-cantu means cockcrow in Latin **(75)**. We also grouped together in prayer in a small dungeon thought to be where Jesus spent time prior to his Via Dolorosa. We made our way across the street and entered the Old City through Zion Gate to visit the Upper Room which commemorates where Jesus shared the Passover (Last Supper) with his disciples and instituted the Eucharist. "And during supper Jesus, knowing that the Father had given all things into his hands, and that he had come from God and was going to God, got up from the table, took off his outer robe, and tied a towel around himself. Then he poured water into a basin and began to wash the disciples' feet and to wipe them with the towel that was tied around him" (John 13:3-5, New Revised Standard Version Catholic Edition).

While they were eating, Jesus took a loaf of bread, and after blessing it, he broke it, gave it to the disciples, and said, "Take, eat; this is my body."

Then he took a cup, and after giving thanks he gave it to them, saying, "Drink from it, all of you; for this is my blood of the covenant, which is poured out for many for the forgiveness of sins. (Mathew 26: 26-28, New Revised Standard Version Catholic Edition). Jesus, then concludes the Passover with "I give you a new commandment, that you love one another. Just as I have loved you, you also should love one another. By this everyone will know that you are my disciples, if you have love for one another" (John 13:34-35, New Revised Standard Version Catholic Edition). Wow, the Last Supper was filled with epic events and also foretells His betrayal and Peter's denial.

I was fascinated and enamored by the only piece of artwork in the Upper Room. An image of a mother pelican with her chicks is carved into the capital on top of a pillar at the Cenacle, the Upper Room on Mount Zion in Jerusalem, where tradition holds that Jesus shared the Last Supper with his apostles and instituted the Eucharist. It is the only artwork in the entire room, and it is singularly appropriate because it is a symbol for Jesus and the Eucharist. "Christians see parallels between the mother pelican and her chicks and Jesus and his followers. The mother pelican represents Jesus, the chicks represent us. The chicks dwell in the safety of the nest, believers dwell in the safety of the

Church. The mother is the head of the nest, and Jesus is the head of the Church (Eph 1:22). The mother has an intense concern for her chicks and it goes against her nature to allow any of them to perish, and Jesus has a great love for us and wants none of us to perish.

When food is in short supply, the pelican pierces its breast with its sharp, pointed beak, and the side of Jesus was pierced by a sharp, pointed lance (John 19:34a). Blood flows from the pelican's breast, and blood flowed from Jesus' side (John 19:34b). The mother's blood is drink for her chicks, and the blood of Jesus is 'true drink' (John 6:55b). The mother gives her life that her chicks might live, and Jesus laid down His life that we might live (John 15:13). The mother's blood saves the lives of the chicks, and the blood of Jesus is salvation and eternal life (John 6:54) for those who receive it. Because of these striking similarities, the mother pelican and her chicks have come to represent the Eucharist, as well as redemption and salvation" **(76)**.

Our last stop for the day was a short bus ride to Ein Karem and to the Church of the Visitation. Outside the church is a large wall filled with Magnificat translations in numerous languages. The Magnificat is referred to as the Canticle or Song of Mary as she is greeted by her cousin Elizabeth. And

Mary said: "My soul glorifies the Lord, and my spirit has rejoiced in God my Savior. For He has regard for the humble bondservant; for behold, from now on all generations will call me blessed. For the Mighty One has done great things for me; and Holy is His name. And His mercy is to every generation toward those who fear Him. He has done mighty deeds with His arm; He has scattered those who were proud in the thoughts of their hearts. He has brought down rulers from their thrones and has exalted those who were humble. He has filled the hungry with good things and sent the rich away empty-handed. He has given help to His servant Israel, in remembrance of His mercy, just as He spoke to our fathers, to Abraham and his descendants forever." Mary stayed with her about three months, and then returned to her home (Luke 1:46-56).

While inside the Church of the Visitation, a large and colorful mural depicts the Holy Spirit's descent on Mary and Elizabeth and the infant jumps for joy! "And it came to pass that when Elizabeth heard the salutation of Mary, the infant leaped in her womb. And Elizabeth was filled with the Holy Spirit" (Luke 1:41). That infant was John the Baptist, the one anointed to prepare the way for Jesus Christ. Timing is everything and as a bonus we were invited to listen to a priest record a song in Italian. His voice rivaled the famous opera singer, Luciano Pavarotti. As we returned to the bus, I stopped once again at Mary's Spring where the *Godcident* occurred with the Jewish woman weeks ago. I thanked the Lord for that encounter and splashed some cold spring water onto my face. Water is life!

We returned in time to refresh prior to 6:30 p.m. mass and then went to our pilgrimage farewell supper on the rooftop of the Notre Dame Center. "In French, Notre Dame means 'Our Lady'. In 1882, a large group of pilgrims began coming to the Holy Land under the direction of French Assumptionists. The experience gained from their pilgrimages prompted the religious to build a center to host French pilgrims. The location of the new center would be right next to the walls of the Holy City of Jerusalem and would be known as Notre Dame de France. Pilgrims have enjoyed the amenities of the Notre Dame Center over the last 130 years spoiled only by periods of war and conflict" **(77)**.

Our rooftop gathering was certainly a highlight of our pilgrimage to give glory, praise, and honor to God and to celebrate this blessed event with one another. This open-air venue overlooked East Jerusalem and the view was magnificent, especially at night. The Temple Mount and Dome of the Rock were illuminated and quite remarkable. The steak and salmon entrees were prepared to perfection and Team Love God was busy handing out prints of photos to each family unit capturing a special Holy Land moment. As this joyous celebration came to an end, I was moved by the Holy Spirit to make one last visit to the Old City and the Western Wall.

I walked down to this holy site with a long procession of Jews on the evening of Shabbat-the Jewish day of rest. I felt a welcome closeness to the young Jewish men whom I engaged in conversation on our fifteen-minute walk from the City Center to the Western Wall. At one point they asked me my religion and with a big smile, I proudly proclaimed, "I worship and love the perfect Jew." They smiled and jokingly said, "Who is that?" This provided me the opportunity to boldly proclaim, "Jesus Christ!"

As I entered through security, I anticipated a large mass of worshippers, and I was not disappointed. With cat-like agility, I weaved through the mass of humanity present. The Holy Spirit guided me to the northwestern corner of the Western Wall, considered by many to be the most holy place. The Holy Spirit opened a lane for me, and I was soon in position. The Jews around me were very polite and friendly. I was a Christian amongst a sea of Jews. As they were singing songs in Hebrew, I sang two songs that I wrote, "Talk to Jesus, my guiding light" in English and "Jesus Sana" (Jesus Heals) in Spanish.

After singing for ten minutes, I noticed the singing around me was quieter. As I opened my eyes and looked around, there was no Jew within ten meters of me. Was my singing that bad or did the powerful name of Jesus create this separation? I smiled, looked up to the heavens and silently whispered, "that was you Jesus." My Crazy for Christ moment at the Western Wall was the perfect end to my 50-day Pentecost in the Holy Land.

CHAPTER 28

ON THE ROAD TO EMMAUS, OUR FINAL DAY AND HOME SWEET HOME!

On our last day of the pilgrimage, we visited the ruins at Emmaus and one of the most touching of Christ's post-resurrection appearances. We celebrated mass under a canopy and received the Eucharist in this open-air chapel. The small museum was ordained with mosaics and historical information that summarized the timeline of the significant events in the Holy Land. I was enamored by the mural of Jesus, the mosaic of birds, the colorful flowers and lush vegetation. There was an opportunity for a photo with Jesus and Cleophas walking the road to Emmaus. Cleopas was one of the two disciples whom Jesus joined on the road to Emmaus during the afternoon of the day of His Resurrection. They did not recognize Jesus at first. Then one of them, named Cleopas, answered him, "Are you the only visitor to Jerusalem who does not know the things that have happened there in these days" (Luke 24:18)?

Jesus accepted their invitation to eat with them and as He broke the bread and as He handed it to them, their eyes were "opened" to recognize Jesus and He vanished. So, who is the unknown disciple? I believe this powerful story invites each one of us to claim our inheritance as sons and daughters (disciples) of the Most High Jesus Christ walking with Jesus on the path to salvation. You and I are the unknown disciple!

We returned for lunch at the Notre Dame Center for our farewell luncheon and goodbyes. We all looked photogenic in our group picture standing outside in front of the Notre Dame Center. A few pilgrims departed for the airport to catch earlier flights. Most of us were leaving at midnight for the eleven-hour flight to New York City. I walked with a few pilgrims to show them the Garden Tomb outside the Damascus Gate and leisurely walked through the Old City for the last time. And guess who God wanted me to say goodbye to one more time? There was Sister Frida from the St. Joseph School. God blessed me with one more opportunity to attend mass at the Notre Dame Center, sing in the choir, and read the intentions on the Feast of St. John the Baptist.

We boarded the bus at 7:30 p.m. for the forty-five-minute bus ride to the Ben Gurion International Airport in Tel Aviv. Since we were traveling during Shabbat the traffic was extremely light. My check in was smooth and easy, and I meandered to the food court and purchased a tomato-cheese-eggplant sandwich. I slept seven hours of the eleven-hour flight from Tel Aviv to New York City and what a *Godcident*. I awoke refreshed for the next leg of my journey to Dallas-Fort Worth. In Dallas, I had a seven-hour layover and the United Services Organization (USO) lounge for active-duty military and retirees is a welcome pitstop. "There are over fifty airport USO lounges internationally with free snacks, coffee, tea, water and soft drinks and comfy chairs to take a quick nap. Most locations feature televisions, video game systems and free Wi-Fi so visitors can use their own devices to check in with loved ones back home. The USO is an American nonprofit-charitable corporation that provides live entertainment, such as comedians, actors and musicians, social facilities, and other programs to members of the United States Armed Forces and their families. Since 1941, it has worked in partnership with the Department of War, and later with the Department of Defense (DoD), relying heavily on private contributions and on funds, goods, and services from various corporate and individual donors. Although it is congressionally chartered, it is not a government agency." **(78)**.

Prior to boarding my flight to Rapid City, I sated my appetite with Texas barbeque complete with sausage, beans, potato salad, collard greens and topped off with peach cobbler. I was then prepared to sleep on the two-hour flight home and sleep I did. I am blessed to have a great neighbor in Chuck who picked me up at the airport and delivered me to my doorstep at 10:00 p.m. I was soon asleep and grateful for the blessings of the Lord on my Holy Land adventure.

CHAPTER 29

MY "HOLY MOMENTS" IN THE HOLY LAND

Officially, I spent fifty-three days in the Holy Land. During my 50-day Pentecost in the Holy Land, God blessed me with wisdom, strength, health, and perseverance. I felt the presence of the Holy Spirit guiding me throughout. Undoubtedly, I will return to continue my work as a missionary disciple to spread the gospel message of salvation through healthcare all for the glory of God. This experience was the culmination of our Shmita or "year to give". I am most confident that God will continue to guide me as an "anointed" disciple to continue His work on earth all for His glory. Indeed, the best is yet to come...

Please let me share my five most sacred moments during my fifty-day Pentecost in the Holy

Land in no specific order. First, our mercy night at the Duc in Altum chapel was a powerful, healing experience. Second, my celebration of Pentecost in the Occupied West Bank was filled with the power of the Holy Spirit. Third, our prayer for one another at the Pools of Bethesda was a tremendous gesture of love, kindness, and compassion. Fourth, the powerful name of Jesus displayed in song at the Western Wall during my last night in the Holy Land was monumental. Indeed, what a powerful name it is, the name of Jesus Christ, our King! Lastly, the Holy Spirit inspired epiphany to the complex and contentious problem in the Holy Land while I was floating on my back in the Dead Sea. The simple answer to this complex problem is love, for God is love. It is your "Love God logo." Offer to put your "Love God logo" on the flag of "The Holy Land."

CHAPTER 30

GOD IS LOVE

So, the answer is "God is Love." My experience in the Holy Land amongst us common people: Jews, Muslims, Christians, and Druze is that we all love the same God and desire peace within the "Holy Land." We all are descendants of Abraham, share a common lineage, and glorify the same God. While floating on my back in the Dead Sea on June 21, 2023, the Holy Spirit whispered to me the solution for peace in the Holy Land. The solution to a complex problem was quite enlightening…God is Love!

This "Love God logo" is to be the symbol on the flag of The Holy Land. "God is Love" is universally accepted by the Judaism, Islam and Christianity. As Madji so eloquently professed in Chapter 11: "One country called 'The Holy Land' with open borders. This country is for all people. We must be able to sit at the table as equals in truth, honor, and respect. Honor and respect are the highest forms of love. Then, and only, can we come together as brothers and sisters serving God." I believe it is through God's chosen people, the Jews, that he expects them to lead with love.

Many are called but few are chosen. The January 28, 2024, Green Olive Collective Newsletter highlights Benzion Sanders is clearly chosen as a veteran of the Israeli Defense Force (IDF) serving in the Gaza Strip in 2014. His military service motivated him to become an activist against occupation and convinced him that the violence of military rule must end. In the October 28, 2023, edition of *The New York Times,* Benzion wrote an Opinion Guest Essay titled, "I fought for the IDF in Gaza. It made me fight for peace." Benzion's experience in Operation Protective Edge helped him realize that Israeli policies of siege, closure, bombardment, and ground invasion have not brought anyone closer to a future of dignity and security. "He is the Jerusalem Director of Extend Programs and the former Jewish Diaspora Education Coordinator of Breaking the Silence, an organization of former soldiers who served in the Israeli military since the start of the Second Intifada and take it upon themselves to expose the public to the reality of life under occupation."

As a former U.S. Army soldier, U.S. Air Force and Public Health physician with 26 years of creditable active-duty service, I was blessed to put "boots" on the ground for 53 days in the Holy Land. I wholeheartedly agree with Benzion that the violence of military rule must end. In my Holistic Health and Healing ministry our mission of love and forgiveness is our movement as we strongly advocate for honor, respect, and peace amongst all people. Veterans strongly resonate with the famous quote from Albert Campus, "Peace is the only battle worth waging."

We acknowledge and salute all veterans as so eloquently stated by the late Buddhist monk, Thich Nhat Han: "Veterans are the light at the tip of the candle illuminating the way for the whole nation. If Veterans can achieve awareness, transformation, understanding, and peace…they can teach us how to make peace with ourselves and each other, so we never have to use violence to resolve conflicts again."

As we pray for a peaceful solution to the violence in the Holy Land and other areas of conflict, Moses speaks this passage from Deuteronomy to remind us that God's roadmap to peace and prosperity is through the love of God and each other.

And now, Israel, what does the Lord, your God, ask of you but to fear the Lord, your God, and follow his ways exactly, to love and serve the Lord, your God, with all your heart and all your soul, to keep the commandments and statutes of the Lord, which I enjoin on you today for your own good. Think! The heavens, even the highest heavens, belong to the Lord, your God, as well as the earth and everything on it. Yet in love for your fathers the Lord was so attached to them as to choose you, their descendants, in preference to all other peoples, as indeed he has now done.

Circumcise your hearts, therefore, and be no longer stiff-necked. For the Lord, your God is the God of gods, the Lord of lords, the great God, mighty and awesome, who has no favorites, accepts no bribes; who executes justice for the orphan and the widow, and befriends the alien, feeding and clothing him. So you too must befriend the alien, for you were once aliens yourselves in the land of Egypt. The Lord, your God, shall you fear, and him shall you serve; hold fast to him and swear by his name. He is your glory, he, your God (Deuteronomy 10:12-21, NIV).

“When an alien lives with you in your land, do not mistreat him. The stranger who lives as a foreigner with you shall be to you as the native-born among you, and you shall love him as yourself; for you lived as foreigners in the land of Egypt. I am Yahweh, your God (Leviticus 19:34, NIV). Do not forget to show hospitality to strangers, for by doing so some people have shown hospitality to angels without knowing it” (Hebrews 13:2, NIV).

In Exodus Chapter 20, God gave Moses the ten commandments out of love for His chosen people to demonstrate His absolute righteousness through the promised Messiah. The rewards for loving God and following His commandments extend to a thousand generations. It really is that simple.

“You shall not bow down to them or worship them; for I, the LORD your God, am a jealous God, punishing the children for the sin of the parents to the third and fourth generation of those who hate me, but showing love to a thousand generations of those who love me and keep my commandments” (Exodus 20:5-6, NIV). And how do we gather as equals at the table? First, you set a place for God at the table. Start in prayer giving glory, honor and praise to Almighty God. Acknowledge the divine power of God’s presence. Create a culture of kindness. Forgiveness is love in action. Love your neighbor. Befriend the alien. Be the change that you want to see in the world. Be the person that you want to meet. Break the generational bonds of brokenness and bondage and replace them with the generational strength of love and forgiveness. When you have the choice to love or to be right, choose to love and you will always be right!

As shared in Chapter fifteen, the last paragraph of Bishop Riah's book, *Caught in Between* ends with: "We have yet to discover who will be our Good Samaritan. We continue to pray for him-and like the wounded man we may have to wait for a stranger, someone not of our own, to fill the role." After much prayer and discernment, I texted Bishop Riah, "I am the Good Samaritan." When God picks you, God equips you. When you lead with love, God multiplies and blesses your efforts. The message in this book is a pebble in the pond to create a tsunami of love throughout the world in preparation for God's plan to save Israel.

CHAPTER 31

GOD'S PLAN FOR ISRAEL IS IRREVOCABLE

Biblically we know that God's plan for Israel is unchanging and His call to action is irrevocable. God chose the Jews to be His special people and He will never leave nor forsake them. God is firmly in control of His salvation plan for the Jews.

> God's plans for the earth and humanity are in motion. His purposes are clear and never coincidental. But to understand God's heart for mankind, we must acknowledge the unique role God gave to His people Israel. Because His love knows no bounds and is never changing, the covenant-keeping God of Abraham, Isaac, and Jacob watches carefully over

all the nations. A significant leg of His journey with mankind has been in the land of Israel. There, He walked with Abraham. He revealed His laws to Moses. And He sent His Son to this same geographical space in Jewish flesh.

In the first verse of Isaiah 53 we see that Israel, for the most part, would reject the Messiah who came to die for her sins. Yet, a future salvation of Israel is promised by God. The day is coming when the eyes of the Jewish people will be opened to see in living color that Jesus of Nazareth is their only Messiah and Savior. Most of the church today is ignorant of this awesome mystery. Even Paul needed to say to the Roman church in Romans chapter 11:26, 'And then all Israel will be saved!' In these verses Paul uses several key words to prove that God plans to reveal Himself to Israel. Paul speaks of the people of Israel as the recipients of God's election, gifts, and calling—which 'are irrevocable.' And not one of those terms speaks of their future redemption as dependent on Israel's worthiness or merit.

Blindness has come upon part of Israel until the full number of Gentiles enter in, and then all Israel will be saved (Romans 11:25-26). God gave the Israelites a spirit of stupor; blind eyes and deaf ears, and it is so to this day (V.8). 'I further ask, does their stumbling mean that they are forever fallen? Not at all' (V.11)! The unbelief of Israel has paved the way for the preaching of the gospel to the Gentiles and for their easier acceptance of it outside of Jewish culture. In God's design it should follow that Israel's ultimate acceptance of the gospel message will benefit the world even more than its original unbelief.

The apostle Paul sums up Israel's final conversion through the triumph of God's mercy. 'Out of Zion will come the deliverer who shall remove all impiety from Jacob; and this is the covenant I will make with them when I take away their sins. In respect to the gospel, the Jews are enemies of God for your sake; in respect to the election, they are beloved by him because of the patriarchs. God's gifts and his call are irrevocable' (VV. 26-29).

> This has been God's plan all along. Israel's unbelief is being utilized to grant the light of faith to the gentiles. Meanwhile, Israel remains dear to God, still the object of His special providence, the mystery of which will one day be revealed. God's gifts and His call are irrevocable! In John 4:22, Jesus reminds us that salvation is from the Jews (79).

"Neither rebellion nor war cure wounds or tears, neither do they undo chains. To live as just people does all that. Then God intervenes" **(80)**. When kindness and truth meet, justice and peace shall kiss (Psalm 85:10, NIV). We serve a powerful God, and it is a compliment when we ask big things of Him! All we have to do to fix the world is to love one another, so let's lead with love as the power of love is God!

ABOUT THE AUTHOR

Dr. George J. Ceremuga is an Osteopathic Family Physician who practices Holistic Health and Healing. He is the author of *God Loves the Children*, *Lead with Love Daily Devotions,* and *All for the Glory of God* daily inspirations. God never intended medicine nor the path to salvation to be complicated or messy. We have the power to unite all in love, for God is love. This is our choice. We were made by God, for God, and to return to God.

ALSO AVAILABLE FROM

Dr. George J. Ceremuga

Through the eyes of a child, **"God Loves the Children"** inspires the reader to be empowered to live fully alive in mind, body, and spirit.

Scan the QR and grab your copy today!

amazon **amazon**kindle

ALSO AVAILABLE FROM

Dr. George J. Ceremuga

Learn more how to live fully alive in mind, body, and spirit with our **free interactive workbook**.

Scan the QR to accessthe free complimentary workbook.

ALSO AVAILABLE FROM

Dr. George J. Ceremuga

We are blessedto inspire others through our **Lead with Love 365 Daily Devotion** book. What a beautiful way to begin a new day, reading these inspiring devotions and reflections of life.

Scan the QR and grab your copy today!

amazon **amazon**kindle

ALSO AVAILABLE FROM

Dr. George J. Ceremuga

"My 50-Day Pentecost in the Holy Land" is not just a chronicle of travels; it's an odyssey of the soul, a captivating testament to the transformative power of faith and the Pentecostal experience in one of the world's most revered landscapes.

Scan the QR and grab your copy today!

amazon kindle

ALSO AVAILABLE FROM

Dr. George J. Ceremuga

'All for the Glory of God' Daily Inspirations reminds us that each day is a new beginning. When God blessesus with another day, that is His gift to us. What is our gift to Him?

Scan the QR and grab your copy today!

amazon kindle

REFERENCES

(1) What Is the Geography of the Holy Land Like? - Community in Mission (adw.org)

(2) Israel Summary | Britannica

(3) Tower of David Museum - Visit Israel Visit Israel

(4) Tower of David Museum - Visit Israel Visit Israel

(5) Western Wall in Jerusalem | Tourist Israel

(6) Church of All Nations « See The Holy Land

(7) The Jerusalem Post, March 21, 2021

(8) Saxum – The Saxum Visitor Center helps pilgrims to deepen their knowledge of the Holy Land through different multimedia resources in order to enrich each person's Holy Land experience.

(9) Bethlehem - Tourist Israel

(10) Pro Terra Sancta | Associazione no profit in Terra Santa

(11) West Bank | History, Population, Map, Settlements, & Facts | Britannica

(12) Nablus | Map, Meaning, & Soap | Britannica

(13) Nablus | Friends of the Holy Land

(14) Nablus | Map, Meaning, & Soap | Britannica

(15) I Will Die to Protect This Holy Well in the West Bank (vice.com)

(16) shavuot and pentecost relationship - Search (bing.com)

(17) Maria C. Khoury "Christina goes to the Holy Land"

(18) Saint George Greek Orthodox Church Taybeh Christina Childrens Books Page (saintgeorgetaybeh.org)

(19) St George and the Holy Land - ONE FOR ISRAEL Ministry

(20) What is the significance of Jericho in the Bible? | GotQuestions.org

(21) A guide to Wadi Rum, Jordan (nationalgeographic.com)

(22) A Guide to Petra, Jordan (nationalgeographic.com)

(23) The Complete One Day Petra Guide (+FREE Trail Map) · Travel Surf Repeat

(24) Makor HaTikvah (kehila.org)

(25) Little Hearts Pre-School, Abigail (kehila.org)

(26) About - Anglican International School Jerusalem (aisj.co.il)

(27) The Eucharist | USCCB

(28) 'The Jesus guy': Bearded man who has become familiar sight in Jerusalem wearing a robe and carrying a cross revealed to be a Detroit preacher | Daily Mail Online

(29) The Significance of Shabbat | My Jewish Learning

(30) Agriculture in Israel - Wikipedia

(31) Nazareth - Wikipedia

(32) Riah Abu El-Assal "Caught in Between" The Extraordinary Story of an Arab Palestinian Christian Israeli

(33) Abu El-Assal, p 154.

(34) Nazareth Village | About - Nazareth Village

(35) Understanding The Significance of The Olive Tree and Anointing Oil | Joseph Prince Ministries

(36) Understanding The Significance of The Olive Tree and Anointing Oil | Joseph Prince Ministries

(37) Understanding The Significance of The Olive Tree and Anointing Oil | Joseph Prince Ministries

(38) Understanding The Significance of The Olive Tree and Anointing Oil | Joseph Prince Ministries

(39) What Is Za'atar and How Do You Use It? (allrecipes.com)

(40) Dream Catcher | History, Origin, Meaning & Indian Symbolism - PowWows.com

(41) The Sea of Galilee | Israel's Harp-Shaped Lake | Touchpoint Israel

(42) The Golan Heights Meaning in the Bible and for Israel — FIRM Israel

(43) Golan Heights | History, Map, & Facts | Britannica

(44) The Golan Heights Meaning in the Bible and for Israel — FIRM Israel

(45) Mount Bental | Tourist Israel

(46) Druze in Israel | My Jewish Learning

(47) Kibbutz Ein Gev - Tourist Israel

(48) Yardenit Baptismal Site on the Jordan River, Sea of Galilee | HolyLandSite.com

(49) The changing generations of Syrians in Israel - The

Jerusalem Post (jpost.com)

(50) Tel Megiddo National Park - Israel Nature and Parks Authority

(51) Saint John Bosco | Biography, Early Life, Magician, Patron Saint, Feast Day, & Facts | Britannica

(52) The Church of the Holy Sepulchre - Medieval Studies - Oxford Bibliographies

(53) Damascus Gate: The significance of the main entry into Jerusalem's Old City | Middle East Eye

(54) A site of Christian worship & witness in Jerusalem - The Garden Tomb

(55) What is the Point of a Pilgrimage? | Simply Catholic

(56) Father Anthony Sortino, LC, Holy Land Pilgrimage- A Practical Guide and Spiritual Resource to Experience the Holy Land, 4th edition, pages 32-33.

(57) What is Fresco Painting? Exploring the Ancient Art of Painting on Plaster (mymodernmet.com)

(58) Shepherds' Field « See the Holy Land

(59) Grotto of the Nativity « See the Holy Land

(60) Milk Grotto « See the Holy Land

(61) Duc in altum – Magdala Tourist Center

(62) Tabgha - Tourist Israel

(63) Mount of Beatitudes « See the Holy Land

(64) Attractions Magdala, Tiberias - The Magdala Hotel

(65) Huntsmans in the Holy Land: Holy Land Day 2: Valley of the Doves, St. Peter's Primacy, Tabgha, and Caesarea Philippi

(66) What Are the Dead Sea Scrolls? - Biblical Archaeology Society

(67) Western Wall in Jerusalem | Tourist Israel

(68) Bar Mitzvah: When It Is and How to Celebrate - What you need to know about reaching the age of bar mitzvah - Chabad.org

(69) https://www.chabad.org/library/article_cdo/aid/1912609/jewish/Bar-Mitzvah-When-It-Is-and-How-to-Celebrate.htm

(70) Dome of the Rock summary | Britannica

(71) Church of St Anne « See the Holy Land

(72) Church of Pater Noster « See the Holy Land

(73) Israel Museum, Jerusalem - Tourist Israel

(74) Church of Dominus Flevit « See the Holy Land

(75) Church of St Peter in Gallicantu « See the Holy Land

(76) Why the pelican with chicks is a symbol of the Eucharist - TheCatholicSpirit.com

(77) Notre Dame of Jerusalem - History (notredamecenter.org)

(78) United Service Organizations - Wikipedia

(79) God's Plan: The Role of Israel in Scripture for Us — FIRM Israel

(80) Maria Valtorta, The Poem of the Man-God, Volume I, page 460.

Made in the USA
Middletown, DE
20 September 2024

60720633R00137